HOME AT LAST

ENDURING DESIGN FOR
THE NEW AMERICAN HOUSE

HOME AT LAST

ENDURING DESIGN FOR
THE NEW AMERICAN HOUSE

GIL SCHAFER III

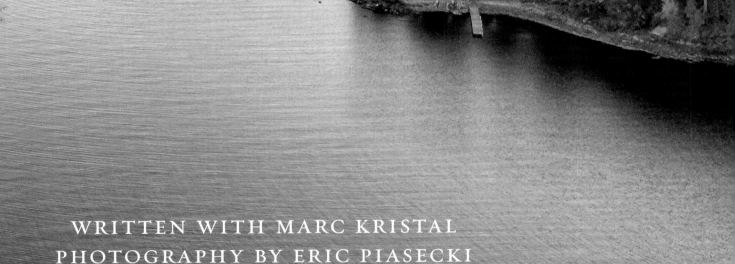

WRITTEN WITH MARC KRISTAL
PHOTOGRAPHY BY ERIC PIASECKI

RIZZOLI
NEW YORK

New York · Paris · London · Milan

For Courtnay, Bankes, and Bennett—
My home, at last.

CONTENTS

INTRODUCTION

This is my third outing as an author in a bit more than a decade's time—following *The Great American House* (2012) and *A Place to Call Home* (2017)—and each time I sit down to write, I realize how much my life—and my work—have changed since the last time I traded my architect's cap for an author's. So: what is different this time around?

It's a fair question. And while I'd like to answer by stating that the projects you will find herein represent a departure from my previous work (which is true), that is not, happily, the whole story. There are, in fact, other compelling reasons to sit at the keyboard once again, having to do with the richness of life experience and the marvelously unexpected directions in which it can send you over time.

When I wrote volumes one and two of what might now be considered a three-part series, it was my genuine belief that they were in large measure about my clients. But *The Great American House* and *A Place to Call Home* were equally concerned with my own personal journey as an architect: how to create classical buildings that "lived modern" and how to adapt what I did to different regions and ways of life, in both cases drawing upon my memories, experiences, education, and life lessons. In short, I think they were probably as much about me as about my clients.

This book is a continuation of that journey—but with the expansion of my own understanding of the lives of those who live in the houses I design. The beauty of the passage of time is that it deepens your discernment through experience. And with time I have gained an ever-expanding appreciation for the fact that a house must never be about its architect, but rather all about those who will live within its walls. This book, then, really is about my clients—which is to say that it's also about you, the reader.

What has been the catalyst for my personal evolution in recent years? Well, most notably, a significant change in my own life, one that set off a chain reaction of experiences (amplified, it must be said, by a global pandemic) that entirely upended my worldview—a development that infused my work with a deepened sensitivity to the intimate character of home and family, and enabled me to tackle ever more complex, challenging projects with confidence and imagination.

In short: I got married. Nobody ever thought I'd do it. Frankly, at some point even *I* thought I'd never do it. But at the not-so-tender age of 57, an incomparable woman welcomed me into her life, I became the stepdad to two teenagers—and my orderly bordering-on-the-fetishistic, perfectly hermetic, always camera-ready single-guy life went utterly out the window. Suddenly my pristine Greek Revival country house had a bright-blue plastic tub—filled with baby ducks!—in the living room, as that's what my stepdaughter wanted as her distraction from covid isolation. Suddenly there was a fifty-gallon dragon lizard tank in the bedroom upstairs—and a monumental gaming computer obscuring my classical columns! Suddenly the hushed environment of my library-like apartment in New York City's Greenwich Village, with its carefully curated collection of stuff, seemed so irrelevant to what was going on in my life.

It had been easy for me to design a house that seemed perfect when nothing ever took place in it that wasn't my idea. But what I have learned, as my life has evolved, is that a house—a *home*—that embraces the glorious mess that is the way we live day-to-day can still be functional, beautiful, and filled with joy. Indeed, a home is in many ways defined by the conflicting, cacophonous agendas that can coexist within it. The acid test, of course, was that not only did I adapt fairly easily to my new condition, I embraced and appreciated it—I was *grateful*.

"You had no idea, did you?" my wife, Courtnay, often jokes. No, I had no idea. But apart from the irreplaceable pleasures of family, this seemingly straightforward middle-aged transformation delivered an unexpected benefit: it deepened my practice of architecture.

These recent years have expanded my understanding of the ways that a home can tell a story about *you*—your family, your passions, your style—and, of course, the story the architect wishes to tell must never interfere with that. My design direction is the means, but never the end, of a house, which is why I say that a project is only a success for me if it's a success for my clients.

I think I have also become a better listener as I have gotten older—a more willing listener, and, consequently, a better translator. Admittedly, this can be tricky, because with experience comes impatience, an awareness that certain gambits are going to fail and it's a waste of time to play them out. Rather, I am better able to know what to listen *for*—what to be attuned to when a client, tossing out suggestions, is really onto something, an idea that's original and personal *and* doesn't violate the essential spirit or character of the house they want. Listening humbly and with

PAGE 8: Life before Courtnay: my bachelor apartment, in a nineteenth-century townhouse in Manhattan's West Village, with its carefully curated selection of things I have collected over the years. As it was on the parlor floor, it had 13-foot-high ceilings that easily accommodated the tall neoclassical bookcase, executed in mahogany, that I designed for the living room. ABOVE: A recent family adventure with Courtnay and her two children, our new family together. OPPOSITE: Another view of my old living room. The scagliola—plaster that's been cast in an ancient technique to mimic black marble—fireplace was based on a design by Asher Benjamin.

RIGHT: Conceived in its entirely by my talented interior-designer wife, our new apartment features an entry hall with walls finished in swamp-green lacquer, then waxed to further absorb and enrich the light. These serve as an especially luminous ground for the objects and artworks (notably the outsized eighteenth-century English landscape) that we have gathered together, as well as Courtnay's remarkable collection of photography depicting life in the American South.

an open mind produces a house that is at once more in tune with a client's desires and architecturally more complete.

Which is another way of describing a home that endures— what many of my clients have come to describe as their "forever" home. Tasked, increasingly, with designing these residences—for which the essential component is permanence—I've given a lot of thought to the special character of architectural longevity, and find that certain things remain broadly applicable. Perhaps the most indispensable quality of an enduring home is that it is adaptive to the evolution of life—the house can shape-shift, if you will, depending upon a family's needs. Sometimes you're formal, other times relaxed. Sometimes the place overbrims with family, then becomes an empty nest. Sometimes you want to cozy up in a corner, other days you want to throw open the doors and windows and invite in the landscape. A home that lasts forever makes room for all of these opposing impulses, sometimes simultaneously. Let me add that the same sensibility presides at the microlevel. Rooms that endure must transform as the life of a family develops: as children grow older, lifestyles evolve; as working from home becomes escaping the daily grind; as styles change or they become more permanent.

It is also critical, I have found, to build in ways for my firm's clients to form emotional attachments to their homes. Sometimes this means integrating—quite literally—a family's history into the architecture. In one project that you will see, my team and I took physical elements from a preexisting family house, notably a beloved cypress-paneled library, and reconstructed it in the new residence. What better way to sustain an intergenerational connection than to carry the family's old "Christmas tree" room into their next architectural episode?

As you might imagine from my embrace of the timeless, I am deeply allergic to the trendy. Speaking to the moment can be great, and arresting decorative flourishes and dramatic gestures have their place—they're fun. But gimmicks are to be avoided, and especially, in my experience, in a house's bones. Changing a decorative scheme is a very different matter than, say, taking up a floor after two years because it seemed cool and now looks, well, "so two years ago." Slipcovers don't need to endure, but I believe architecture can, and should.

Avoiding trends and tricks, however, does not preclude indulging in fantasy—another essential characteristic of an enduring home design. So many of the people for whom my team and I work come to us with nothing more—and nothing less—than dreams. A dream of living on a lake. Of being surrounded by family. Of having an idiosyncratic garden that's different from the neighbors' maniacally clipped hedges. Of having a nightclub in the basement. Of a Japanese meditation studio, or of a Hamptons escape that more closely resembles the New England houses remembered from childhood. For my interior designer wife, who upended her eighteen-year life in a wonderful house in San Francisco to move with her kids to New York City, her fantasy was to live in a classic "grown-up" Upper East Side Manhattan apartment with traditional décor. And so now we do.

I think I have also been liberated, as I have matured, from the false choice between historic and contemporary architecture. I describe it as such not because there isn't a difference—to be sure, there is, and I remain a practitioner working in the classical and traditional idioms—but because sometimes a project requires that the two coexist, and to be doctrinaire about one's choices is to detract from a home's potential. The great classical architect Thomas Hastings observed, memorably, that "style is the problem solved." In the pages to come you will see, within historic contexts, more contemporary materials, elements, and strategies that resolved—quite elegantly and effectively—challenges that stumped the language of classicism. In fact, decades of practice have taught me that restricting one's palette to tradition in its most perfect form is actually a contravention of history, which is filled with architects who, guided by such considerations as context and precedent, knew when and how far to bend the rules—and bringing the present into the realm of the past is an extension of that. (The same thinking applies, by the way, to that other false choice: fancy versus simple. Either is okay, and both is even better. It all depends upon your comfort zone, and everyone's is different.)

And speaking of comfort zones: In the context of a global pandemic that so constrained our freedom and increased our dependence on technology (which can further narrow our world), finding ways to engage securely and sublimely with the outdoors has, in our lifetime, never mattered more. Thus, making a connection to landscape is now essential in my practice; and so you will also find, in the pages that follow, homes that benefit from a sense of place, that explode the boundaries between inside and outside, and that form natural enclaves of privacy and peace within the larger context of close-at-hand neighbors. Conversely, there is also a project on the coast of Maine—entirely singular in its uniqueness, and a completely new kind of assignment for me—that preserves a nearly hermetic degree of internal privacy, even as it is stitched inextricably into the public circumstances of a community. Mediating between these conditions presented us with an exquisite challenge—architectural, urbanistic, and even maritime—that taxed our ingenuity in the best ways. The point is that life constantly throws curveballs at us, and if, as architects, we can respond thoughtfully, and with an open mind, a beautiful solution can always be found.

This book, in fact, puts on display many such challenges, ones that (if I'm being absolutely honest) might have stumped me even half a decade ago. Partly it is the accumulation of practical experience that has enabled me to execute more complex, varied work. But here, yet again, the life changes I've gathered have proven indispensable. One of the most profound lessons that family life has taught me is that you can handle much more than you imagined if you have a compelling reason to do so—the reason being, of course, that you love your spouse and children and want things to work out. A family, pulling together, can surmount virtually any challenge (as the pandemic has certainly shown us), and that is an understanding I have applied to my architectural family as well. Whether the head-scratcher involved reconciling the promises and restrictions of a difficult site or the complete reconstruction of a compromised historic mansion, our interdependence as a creative team—our commitment to realizing clients' most cherished dreams—helped us pull off, again and again, high-wire feats of design.

While it is my pleasure to share with you, in these pages, what we have accomplished, I would also like to honor the contract I established with my readers in my first two books. Along with

good stories and pretty pictures (and personal reflections), the "How did you do that?" factor lies at the core of all my writing. The practical takeaway—presenting ideas of which you can make use—affords me as much gratification as showing what it is, in the years since last we met, that the firm has achieved.

This book completes a two-decade-long journey for me and my firm, as well as a varied picture of the work we have done over these last twenty years. And one of the most gratifying byproducts of the work over that time has been when our clients write to us. Architects typically get letters or emails only when something has gone wrong, and in the trade we often note, with not a little rue, that if we *don't* hear from a client after a project's conclusion, that's probably a good thing. But I have been most fortunate, sometimes years after the final coat of paint has dried, to receive notes, photos, and even videos about the enduring satisfactions to be derived from my collaborations with families. We are in the business of creating architecture, an often highly technical exercise in problem-solving drenched in a torrent of mundane details. Amidst the daily scrum, one can sometimes lose sight of the fact that we are also in the joy business, laboring to create dwellings that will reward their occupants for a lifetime (and sometimes, in the case of multigenerational properties, even beyond). So those notes that we receive are most welcome. They keep our eye on the sparrow, as the saying goes, and provide the impetus to return, over and over again, to the drafting board—with interest, enthusiasm, and gratitude.

You had no idea, did you?

The great American author Henry Miller observed that the older he got, the less he knew. I'd put it this way: in my case, the older I've gotten, the more I realize how much I still have to learn. And of all the things about which, to borrow my wife's formulation, I had no idea, the most important was the fact that I needed to live life a little more richly than I had before to achieve an ever-deepening understanding of what makes a truly successful home—a forever home. I have embraced the paradox that the best way to do personal work is to bear in mind, always, that it's not about me. I hope you find that maxim in evidence on every page that follows.

THE SUBSTANCE
OF STYLE

The enduring question of style—that is, which one is right for a given project—always presents a challenge. Why should a house look one way as opposed to another? Typically, there are several factors that come into play: Where is the residence-to-be located, and what are the local aesthetic traditions? What do the site, landscape, and climate suggest? And, not least, which style is most appealing to a client, given his or her (or, usually, their) tastes and programmatic requirements? A consideration of these issues, more often than not, leads smoothly to a solution . . . but not always. Sometimes other, harder-to-quantify emotional factors come into play. This project represents a perfect case in point.

Block Island, where the house is located, has always struck me—since I first visited in my early twenties—as possessing a highly distinctive character, one that sets it apart from Nantucket, Martha's Vineyard, and other destinations off the coast of New England. Thanks to the priorities of the year-rounders, golf courses and jet planes are not to be found there, which I think makes the island less of a

A FAMILY COMPOUND
on
BLOCK ISLAND

GRAPHIC   0   5   10   20   40   SCALE

LEGEND

1. MAIN HOUSE
2. GARAGE / GUEST COTTAGE
3. BARN
4. POOL

resort (and less of a playground), and more low-key: devoted to the satisfactions of slow ferry rides, modest entertainments, and the enduring, contemplative pleasures to be found in land, sea, and sky. Indeed, the terrain, crisscrossed by old stone walls, gives the place a severe, rough-hewn quality that brings to mind

PAGE 17: The view from the meadow below the house. The original stone farm walls still crisscross the property. PREVIOUS PAGES: The reconstructed barn overlooks Block Island's famed Great Salt Pond and, beyond it, the Atlantic. OPPOSITE: The house sits atop a plinth developed with landscape designer Deborah Nevins, who also judiciously extracted old trees from the knoll to open up views, leaving the most magnificent specimens in place. ABOVE: A site plan of the property.

the dramatic (and romantic) beauty of rural Ireland. The architecture, too, stands apart: rather than commanding, ornamented mansions built by wealthy nineteenth-century merchants and sea captains, one finds farmsteads that partake of the simple elegance of vernacular and craft, and the homespun joys of the American Shingle Style at its most straightforward. Perhaps most tellingly, the local ethos is expressed by the fact that it can be difficult to gain approval to build. Style is seldom the issue—rather, preserving Block Island's unspoiled, understated scale and character remains of the utmost importance.

This last consideration—blending into the local zeitgeist—was very much top of mind for our clients. In fact, the family enjoyed a considerable history on the island: the wife had summered there since childhood; she and her husband exchanged vows in a local chapel; and when the couple's four children (now grown) were young, they settled into a comfortable but unremarkable house, on an unassuming property, that enabled them to partake more fully of Block Island's pleasures—seasonally, but as the near-natives they'd become. When a sublime sixteen-acre property, on which the buildings had gone derelict, became available, the family saw an opportunity to truly put down roots, in a substantial multigenerational compound that would be nonetheless unpretentious and unobtrusive—a home that might enable the glories of informal indoor/outdoor living, surrounded by panoramic views in all directions.

The property had its own history, one no less meaningful or deep-rooted than the family's. This was embodied by a nineteenth-century barn, sited picturesquely overlooking Block Island's famed Great Salt Pond, that stood as the iconic hub of a view embracing the low, fluid slopes, the expanse of pond, and, in the near distance, the surging Atlantic. So significant was this visual moment in local lore that it had become a de facto landmark, in front of which visitors and locals alike would pose for snapshots at the edge of the road that skirted the property.

My clients were well aware that they were venturing onto a bucolic variant of hallowed ground, and to impose themselves upon it improperly or presumptuously would not only clash with the island's character, but erase a small but significant bit of history. Rather than feeling daunted, however, the couple saw an opportunity: a chance to be good stewards of a place they loved. Treading lightly and respectfully would enable the family not only to create a home, but to contribute meaningfully to Block Island's singular heritage.

I began by walking the land with my clients, along with the couple's decorator (and my longtime friend), Miles Redd, as well as our landscape architect for the project, Deborah Nevins (another close friend and longtime collaborator), to absorb and understand what was there and, crucially, to perceive what should be held sacred and what remained open to reinterpretation. Very quickly Debby, Miles, and I recognized that, though the barn

wasn't the principal structure, it remained the iconic anchor of the entire property, and an appropriate stage setter for a project with multiple components. Originally the plan was to restore this pivotal structure, but because it had deteriorated severely, we chose instead to reconstruct the barn from the ground up, on precisely the same spot and almost exactly as it was—with a few minor yet meaningful interventions. From the road, appropriately, the barn appears to be identical to its predecessor. But on a less visible side, a cross gable was introduced, to bring natural light into the upper level of the interior. Additionally, we drew on the typological tradition of overscaled barn doors to justify the inclusion of large, glazed sliding doors on the building's north and south sides—big panels that pocket away completely, to facilitate abundant, cross-ventilating ocean breezes and perfectly framed vistas, and support the barn's function as an informal family hangout space and de facto pool house.

Reconstruction also afforded the opportunity for some useful upgrading. Prior to reinserting the interior's most arresting feature—the reclaimed wood timber-frame superstructure— we added steel support members, comprehensive weatherproofing, and well-concealed climate-control systems to what had previously been a bare-bones vernacular building. Restoration, when possible, offers the undeniable pleasure of authenticity. But starting from scratch maximizes livability—and, if properly done, with no loss of visual or tactile "history."

Tackling the barn gave us a great deal of satisfaction. But the residence was the main event, and developing the design with our clients proved to be an enriching, iterative process that required careful manipulation of the terrain by Debby and a journey into architectural history by all of us. Sensitive to context and tradition, mindful of Block Island's lack of pretense and emphasis on understatement, my initial sketches conjured a house comprised of plain gabled forms, akin to the preexisting rudimentary farmhouse we'd

OPPOSITE: The wraparound porch at sunset. The dormer directly above, in the primary bedroom, suggests the ways in which the simple elements of the Shingle Style—in this instance, wave-patterned shingles and plain white-painted boards—can be composed to produce interest, animation, and delight.

be replacing. Yet while my clients embraced an ethos of unobtrusive simplicity, they were equally determined to introduce a measure of architectural exuberance that neither went too far nor violated that essential sense of place. Again, I took my cue from the original farmhouse—this time focusing on its shingled skin.

Block Island enjoys a long tradition of shingled houses, weathered to a sublime silvery gray (with either white or natural trim), and that history provided an obvious, even inevitable, aesthetic direction. But we were drawn as well to the Shingle Style as an emblem, famously, of the "American summer," with everything that implied. The architectural historian Vincent Scully was one of the first to appreciate the qualities of the style, highlighting its free, relaxed, generous, and gentle qualities, and pointing out that it was a mode of architecture that was "the most wholly wedded to the landscape," as he noted in his landmark book *The Shingle Style and the Stick Style*. Scully's observations of the style's "simplicity of materials, freedom of space, expression or function," and "lack of pretension" likely capture why it was so perfect for houses that found their best use during the lazy days of summer. I've also thought that although the style emerged in the late nineteenth century, it remains notably modern in the sense that it encourages a picturesque plan—one that derives its shape from a resident's patterns and preferences of use (in other words, the house's function) rather than proscribed ideas of propriety or correctness—and, as a result, it rewards eccentricity and idiosyncrasy. The best shingled houses push out and pull in expressionistically, as a response to lifestyle and circumstance, and rely upon a clean, rhythmic wrapper of shingles to unify the outcome. The result, I think, perfectly accommodates the relaxed summer lifestyle while delivering a notably Northeastern touch of architectural sophistication.

As an architect, it is generally my preference not to try to nudge a historic style into bold new territory, but rather to work with its language in a more subtle way that, when the project is complete, feels as though I've not quite been there. Toward this end, my clients and I considered various precedents for their house, and arrived at the famous Seven Sisters: seven summer retreats located on the eastern end of Long Island and designed in the 1880s by McKim, Mead & White for the developer Arthur Benson (creator of the Brooklyn neighborhood Bensonhurst) and a half dozen of his cronies. What we found especially appealing about this model—and appropriate to my clients' site and their ambitions for it—was that those houses achieved a high degree of expressiveness using a relatively simple vocabulary: a well-distilled language of gables, dormers, shingle patterns, a smattering of unusual millwork, and a palette of decoration that the architects combined and recombined in imaginative, original ways. The Seven Sisters offered a model that didn't cross the line into overly serious or self-important "Architecture," making them the ideal reference point for what we wanted to achieve: a house that seemed like it had always been there, and caused no one to exclaim, "Wow, did you see what they built up on the hill?!"

The five-bedroom, 5,300-square-foot new residence is sited where the preexisting one had been, at the property's high point—but with a notable difference, one devised by the tirelessly inventive Debby Nevins. The old house disadvantageously sat on uneven land—if you walked out the door, you'd tumble down the hill—but enjoyed a cozy sense of place shaped by surrounding stands of mature trees. To open up cones of view, Debby chose to selectively extract some of that vegetation, yet made a place for the new architecture by crafting a plinth of lawn, bordered by stone walls, on which the house could nestle comfortably. The outcome holds past, present, and future in an elegant, effective balance.

As for the house itself, the design derives its visual interest from interventions and gestures that honor the traditions of the style without overwhelming the simplicity of the building's massing and forms. Different shingle patterns and shapes ("fish scales" being a particular favorite of mine) animate the house's skin. Quiet cornices appear above the first-floor windows on the main block. Board formations produce unexpected panel designs.

OPPOSITE: At left, the house's side door leads to the mudroom and kitchen. To the right of the porch, one of the great enduring pleasures of the American summer: an outdoor shower. Bedrooms for the family's boys are tucked behind the dormers above.

ABOVE: The primary suite dormer. The chimney rises from the living room fireplace, piercing the dormer using much the same gambit that McKim, Mead & White deployed in their shingled houses. OPPOSITE: A whimsical abstract sunburst pattern in the pediment, slender Doric columns, and delicate moldings vitalize the entry.

OPPOSITE AND ABOVE: At the door to the entry hall, sidelights and a transom permit
natural illumination; delicately detailed beamwork and paneled walls add an aura of elegance
absent an excess of formality; and pocket doors connect to an oak-paneled study.

PREVIOUS PAGES: Entering the 20-by-30-foot living room from the front hall, the visitor finds a view that extends through the space and across the landscape to the Atlantic. Thanks to the wraparound porch, the room enjoys windows on three sides; the porch shields the indoors from sun and rain and expands the house's usable footprint. RIGHT: The relaxed vibe of summer living means that the kitchen, these days the hub of daily life in a house, is most often open to the living spaces, as is the case here.

RIGHT: The kitchen features cabinetry crafted by Plain English. Set largely below the windows to avoid obstructing the views and very simple in its design, the cabinetry suits the relaxed vibe of the house. Sawn-timber ceiling beams and wide-plank wood floors contribute to the air of informality, as does the island, with its comfortable combination of work and casual dining space. FOLLOWING PAGES: The screened porch, accessed from the kitchen through wide pocketing glass doors, combines sitting and dining areas and can be enjoyed in all seasons (as can the view of the Great Salt Pond). In the cooler months, the screen panels can be exchanged for glass.

RIGHT: The snug library is paneled in white oak, which we left unfinished to keep the color light and the mood relaxed. Over time, the salt air and sunlight will provide a natural patination.

OPPOSITE: The house has only one stair, set in a small side hall, seen here from the entry hall.
ABOVE: The simple tapered, white-painted balusters terminate in a turned newel post capped with a so-called "mortgage button" fashioned from reclaimed nineteenth-century whale ivory.

Gable ends bulge out over windows. An abstract rendering of the sun's rays is carved into the tympanum above the entry portico.

Rather than creating a full-scale second story, which would have made the house too prominent on its knoll-top site, we tucked the upstairs into the roof, using the Shingle Style's tradition of varied, unpredictably placed dormers to bring light (and height) into the rooms and to break up the mass of the roof. Unlike Georgian or Colonial Revival residences, which adhere to rigid rules of composition and proportion, the Shingle Style's forgiving ethos enabled us to create wider, space-expanding dormers where we needed them that were then absorbed into the overall design by the shingled skin.

Within, the interior that we developed in close collaboration with Miles and his team revolves around an expansive living room that serves as the house's heart (and its dramatic introduction: entering via the portico, one looks straight through the space to the ocean). The pleasurable sense of amplitude is enhanced by the living room's openness to the big adjoining kitchen—in contemporary summer-house living, I find that there's little formal distinction between the two—and both rooms communicate with an even larger

screened porch (ideal for bug-free alfresco dining). Further dissolving the distinction between the house's interior and the great outdoors, an L-shaped covered porch borders the living room on its north and west sides. (A smaller covered porch, in front, shades an informal entrance that connects to the mudroom.) Though the residence is relatively modest in size for a multigenerational house, it remains abundant programmatically, with a library/den off the entry hall and a cozy wet bar off the living room, two bedrooms (for girls) on the main floor, a primary suite and two additional bedrooms (for boys) upstairs, and a generous staircase to tie the two floors together. Here, as in other of our residences, we tried whenever possible to craft buffer zones in the form of vestibules between the sleeping and public areas, so as to create transitions that cushion the private rooms, acoustically and physically, from the hubbub.

This house reunited Miles, Debby, and me for the first time since we collaborated twenty years ago on my own house in the Hudson Valley, but it was really Miles who was our guide on this journey, having known and worked with these clients for many years on a number of projects. He understood how they liked to live, and carried that sensibility into this new home—in a way that was at once in tune with what they'd done previously and appropriate to their new circumstances.

While our original plan for the property featured five freestanding structures, as the design evolved and at our clients' recommendation, we collectively edited this vision down to three—a new garage/guest apartment completes the trio. The resulting assemblage accomplishes many things. It provides a home for a family that can be enjoyed for many generations: its accommodations can expand and contract as needed. It honors the architecture of the Shingle Style without overwhelming a site magnificent in its embrace of natural wonders in all directions. And not least, it understands and respects the enduring ethos of Block Island: making a home that honors, and contributes to, a sense of place—but in the most low-key, understated way.

ABOVE: The primary suite's dressing area draws in light via one of the quirky dormers facilitated by the relaxed rules of the Shingle Style. OPPOSITE: The main bedroom gains extra height from a tray ceiling. French doors open onto a balcony that—like all of the house's zones, in and out—embraces a sweeping view.

OPPOSITE: One of the girls' bedrooms, on the first floor, is animated by bright floral wallpaper and Miles Redd's reliably exuberant color palette.
ABOVE: A second-floor boy's room, tucked under the house's eaves.

ABOVE: Deborah Nevins designed the broad, shallow grass steps that
lead down gently from the main house to the fenced pool area.
OPPOSITE: The adjacent entertaining barn serves as a de facto pool house.

RIGHT: Our reconstruction of the original barn features a new cross gable on the building's south side; this enabled us to add height and light to the structure's upper reaches without changing the original west-facing silhouette, much beloved as a local landmark. The large wood barn doors on the building's south and north sides conceal pocketing glass sliders that open the interior, gloriously, to the entirety of the outdoors.

48

ABOVE AND OPPOSITE: The barn's paneling and trusswork, made from salvaged timbers and wood planking, underpin our recreation of the original interior. The enormous sectional and no less impressive dining table make welcoming gestures to large groups of friends and family and serve as relaxed spots to gather.

RIGHT: The barn's mezzanine features
bunk beds custom built into the woodwork;
just beneath it, we installed a large
video screen that drops down for movie
nights. The utilitarian kitchen tucked into
the building's corner has a broad pair
of windows over the sink that open to a
serving counter just outside, while
the balcony on the building's "view"
side is accessed via two sets of large doors,
glass and screen, that can recess into
the walls completely.

52

RIGHT: The carriage house (aka garage), with a guest apartment directly above, stands at a discreet distance from the main residence. One of the original trees, preserved on the site by landscape architect Deborah Nevins, stands just beyond the house. FOLLOWING PAGES: The iconic—and much-beloved by locals and visitors alike—view of the barn, the property's original pond, and its rolling meadows, seen from the public road.

ENGLISH SPEAKING

As the old joke goes, the pizza in America is better than it is in Italy, because we make it with imported cheese while the Italians use domestic. What the joke reveals is that, however appealing the idea of "imported" may be, it only works domestically if (as is the case with pizza) it is introduced into an appropriate context. This may be especially true of residential architecture because, although we can become enamored of buildings we see in the course of foreign travel, at home the style may prove wildly incompatible with the setting into which it is introduced. Though you will find subtle examples of such transpositions in these pages—a New England house in the Hamptons, Caribbean architecture in South Florida—I always approach this kind of project with extra care. A number of "foreign" styles import elegantly and effectively to these shores, perhaps none more easily than classical architecture. But I find that the trick to making this work successfully is to discover a common thread between a design inspiration and its circumstances, one that makes the marriage of the two seem natural and appealing—or, as I often say, inevitable.

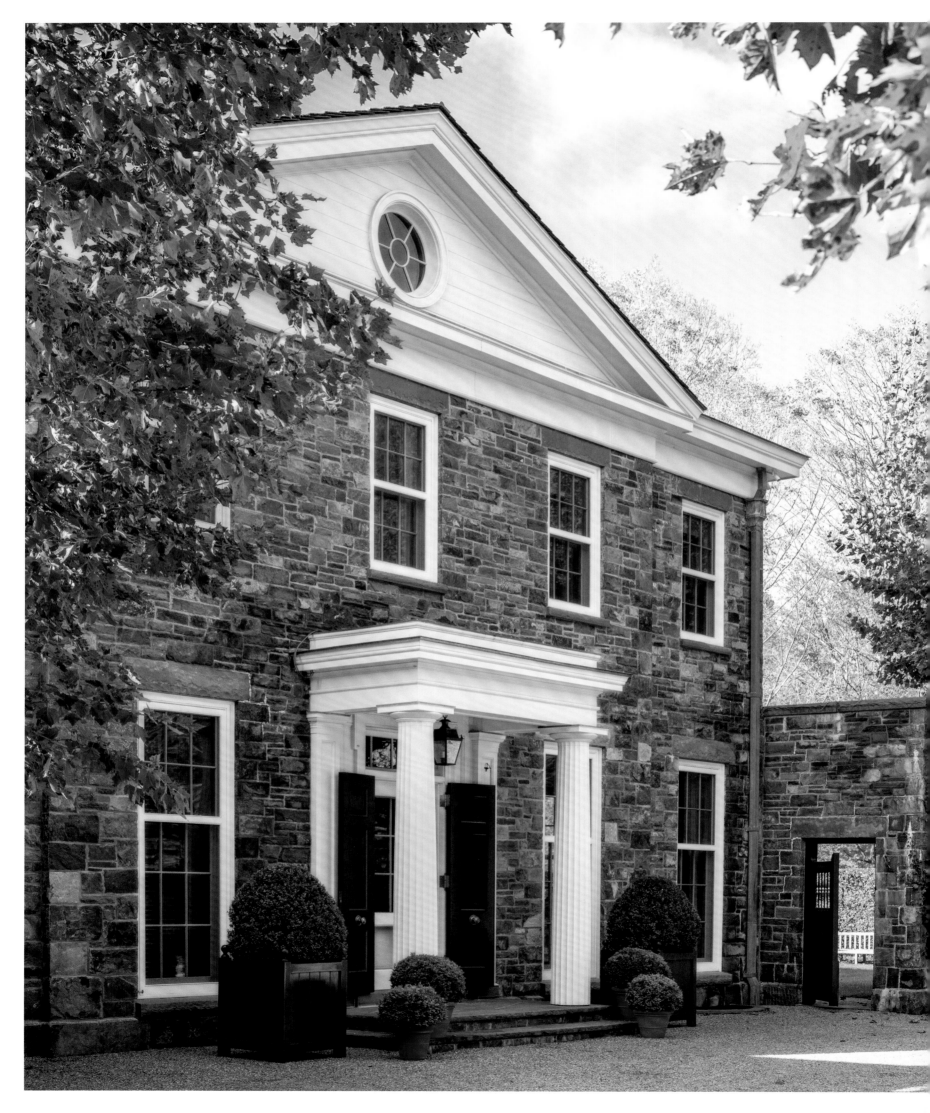

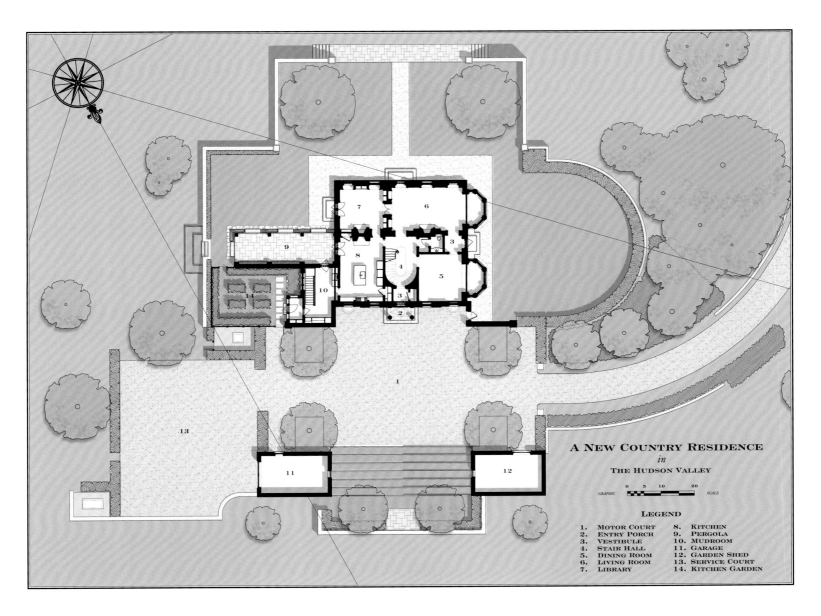

A NEW COUNTRY RESIDENCE
in
THE HUDSON VALLEY

GRAPHIC 0 5 10 20 SCALE

LEGEND

1. MOTOR COURT
2. ENTRY PORCH
3. VESTIBULE
4. STAIR HALL
5. DINING ROOM
6. LIVING ROOM
7. LIBRARY
8. KITCHEN
9. PERGOLA
10. MUDROOM
11. GARAGE
12. GARDEN SHED
13. SERVICE COURT
14. KITCHEN GARDEN

In this instance, my empty-nester clients, a couple who had lived abroad on various continents for many years, acquired a beautiful sixty-acre plot of farmland in a pastoral region of New York's Hudson Valley; their last overseas home had been in Britain, a nest of happy memories and associa-

PAGE 58: The south façade of the house, facing the property's lower meadow, as seen from the entry drive. PREVIOUS PAGES: The house sits at the center of a plinth—a surrounding landscaped precinct, comprised of a suite of garden rooms—that is as much a part of my clients' life as the dwelling itself; each depends upon the other. OPPOSITE: The entry façade, with its Greek Revival details and Doric columns; the native fieldstone was chosen for the balance it achieves between the rustic and the formal. ABOVE: The site plan showing the carefully composed setting of house, gardens, and outbuildings.

tions that they hoped to recreate in some way in their new setting. In some respects, it was an ideal fit: the landscape, with its rolling meadows and fields, hedgerows and stone walls, did indeed evoke the English countryside, and I could see, in my mind's eye, any number of English country estates sitting quite comfortably on a property like this.

Yet rural New York has its own architectural history, and rather than simply landing an English house in Dutchess County, like Dorothy's Kansas house in Oz, I wanted to knit together the aesthetic compatibilities between upstate New York and its British counterparts. During the Regency period, English architecture drew on Grecian precedents, among others, and it occurred to me that this might make an inter-

esting, effective connection to the pronounced and abundant Greek Revival traditions of the Hudson Valley. My other initial thought was to face the residence with fieldstone rather than brick or limestone, both of which struck me as, under the circumstances, too formal and "posh" for this rural setting. My clients' land sits squarely in farm country, and I believed that if we could dress fieldstone with sufficient refinement so that it didn't diminish the classical details of the architecture, the material's relationship to the region's agrarian narrative would tie the house more firmly to its place. In fact, I think the style-and-material gambit proves highly effective. From the moment you arrive, the moldings, proportions, and Doric columns of the Greek Revival entry portico, set against a stately yet rugged fieldstone façade, together produce an effect entirely appropriate to the location, yet maintain a distinctly British character and flavor.

The notion of an English "Palladian" precedent also suggested a cubic structure, rather than a rambling farmhouse, but modest in size and program as befit my clients' needs and circumstances. Nevertheless, I didn't want it to be a boring box devoid of visual interest. As a result, on each façade the stonework alternately recedes and pushes outward in a different way, creating a subtle but vitalizing variation in rhythm and articulation. On the southern elevation, which faces an array of meadows and the property's entrance in the distance, the center flexes inward, producing a "tower" effect at each end; on the western façade, the architecture moves in the opposite direction, pushing outward in the center, with bay windows framing each side of the stonework; and on the house's northern side, the façade pushes forward again in the form of a pedimented front to announce "entry."

Before we could begin to write the house's architectural story, however, we had to solve the considerable challenge of its siting, and this we did with the guiding hand of Deborah Nevins, our landscape designer. The couple understandably wanted to site the house at the property's highest point, a vantage offering hundred-mile views in multiple directions. Debby, however, raised several exceedingly valid points: As

the peak lay at the top of a necklace of steeply sloping meadows, there was in fact no place to put the house—we would need to build a significant level plinth of land on which to set the house and its gardens, a complicated effort of earth-moving and wall-building that would be onerously expensive. Moreover, reaching the house would require creating an elaborate switchback drive that would consume (and blight) the entire hillside, itself an enormous investment (to say nothing of the cost of plowing it each winter).

Hearing this, my clients, I could see, were crestfallen. And I could relate: I, too, had tried to build a house on sloping land not too far from their property, with the same ambition to set it on the highest point, and had been dissuaded from doing so by Debby, for the same reasons. Then and now, I remembered Frank Lloyd Wright's wise observation that if you set your house below your property's peak, you will always have someplace exciting to walk. Debby also offered an intriguing alternative: there was a bit of a bench of land partway up the slope—high enough to afford significant vistas, yet at an elevation that could be accessed via a reasonably brief, relatively flat drive. We could all see that this made a lot more sense as a building site, and with minimal panoramic sacrifice. My pragmatic clients blessed the idea, and we were ready to begin.

Whereas many houses hatched in our office tend to be picturesque in plan, often long and thin to permit natural light and views on two (and sometimes three) sides, with wings and bump-outs that give a certain experiential richness to the rooms inside, this one would be foursquare and thus somewhat inward-looking. This meant that the landscape around the house would have to supply what its architecture could not: an extension of the indoor experience out into the landscape through a series of garden "rooms." Indeed, in this circumstance, the "architecture" of the landscape was essential to completing the architecture of the house.

This indoor/outdoor interdependence first reveals itself at the entry court. The front façade is extended outward into the landscape on each side via two tall garden walls—one

concealing a hedged garden, the other the house's mudroom. These walls are mirrored by two matching stone pavilions on the opposite side of the entry court, and together these four elements define the perimeter of the arrival area; the two pavilions also perform the trick of "holding back" the hillside that begins to rise dramatically just above the house's site. Here, Debby created yet another delightful landscape gesture, extending long grass-covered steps between the two pavilions that frame the view and make a gateway to the property's upper regions.

Off the house's western façade, Debby crafted a garden, defined by a curving hedge of eight-foot-tall hornbeam, which forms a pleasant sitting space—often bathed in golden afternoon light—while screening the views of the driveway from the interior of the house. On the house's eastern side, we designed a long, south-facing pergola on stone piers, draped in a canopy of wisteria, which extends out through French doors from the kitchen—our clients' favorite spot for an alfresco meal. And on the house's southern exposure, Debby laid out a simple grass terrace that rises above the

PREVIOUS PAGES: Two stone outbuildings, connected by shallow grass steps, frame the north side of the entry court; the ensemble forms the portal between the house's landscaped precinct and the farm fields rising above. ABOVE: Past the entry court, a parking area is concealed by tall, clipped hornbeam hedges.

PREVIOUS PAGES: The tall curved hedge of the garden on the house's west side conceals the drive from views through the living and dining room bay windows. ABOVE AND OPPOSITE: A compressed vestibule (with a traditional pull-chain English doorbell) gives way to the drama of the two-story stair hall.

meadow on a plinth of the same fieldstone as the house itself and frames its views with a pair of sycamore trees.

While I have been lucky enough, over the years, to persuade my clients of the importance of landscape to a project's completion, too often I see houses in which the landscape was treated as "something that can be done later, when there's more money available." In fact, I'd much rather that a project's architectural scope be pruned back if it means that the exterior can be more fully realized. In this case, the architecture would not have held together at all without the full completion of the property—gardens, walls, and hedges—as both house and garden are inextricably woven together in a single composition. The hedges are clipped to give shape and definition to the outdoor rooms; the pavilions complete the space of the arrival court; and the stone plinth that extends out into the lower meadow allowed us to create a lawn that gives the entire composition a sense of place within what is otherwise a farm field. Fortuitously, our clients needed no convincing, and the outcome is sublimely comprehensive.

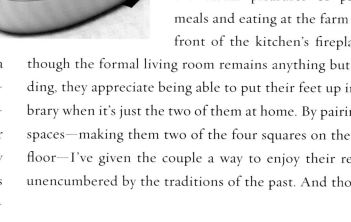

Upon entering the house, you discover a modestly scaled, low-ceilinged vestibule in which a classic English doorbell on a pull chain announces your arrival; a few steps more, and this compression gives way to release: the space expands upward through a two-story stair hall, topped by an ovular laylight that remains particularly English. Many foursquare country houses on the Atlantic's other side have stairs embedded in the interior, and take illumination from above rather than windows, the effect being at once dramatically grand and cozily soothing. As for the stair itself, its sculptural sinuousness is enhanced by its cantilevered character, the way the individual treads project out from the wall, seemingly weightless, as they ascend—mimicking, in wood, the stone treads of an English stair. I particularly love the answering ovals—the floor at bottom, the curves of the stair itself, and the laylight at its peak—that establish the architecture's equipoise, a quality one encounters in many such houses of comparable scale in England.

From the central stair hall, one finds the dining room immediately to the right, and then straight ahead—stretching along the house's southern side, overlooking the lower meadows—the living room, each space with a bay window projecting into the hedged garden to the west. To the left of the stair hall, I set the kitchen and library with a door connecting the two rooms. The latter arrangement is the sort you wouldn't ordinarily find in a house with this level of implied architectural formality—the kitchen, traditionally, would have been hidden off in another wing—but positioning it here, in the heart of the house, is key to living in a modern, comfortable way. My clients are dedicated cooks, and enjoy the casual pleasures of preparing meals and eating at the farm table in front of the kitchen's fireplace, and though the formal living room remains anything but forbidding, they appreciate being able to put their feet up in the library when it's just the two of them at home. By pairing these spaces—making them two of the four squares on the ground floor—I've given the couple a way to enjoy their residence unencumbered by the traditions of the past. And though the

ABOVE AND OPPOSITE: Two views of the oval-shaped stair hall with its cantilevered block treads, mahogany balusters and banister, and cream-and-black limestone floor. The ovular skylit laylight, not pictured, brings light (and drama) into the windowless space.

ABOVE AND OPPOSITE: The dining room, directly off the stair hall, is filled with some of the antique furniture and paintings my clients brought back with them from their multiyear sojourn in England. The architecture reflects the furnishings' formality and serves as an appropriate showcase. The door to the kitchen, across the hall from the dining room and at the bottom of the stairs, is just out of view.

A grand piano fills the bay at the living room's western end; the windows at left look south across the property's lower meadows. The space, though most "proper," is warm and welcoming, thanks in part to the glowing yellow walls and expanse of apple matting on the floor, the result of a lively collaboration between the owners and decorator Thomas Jayne.

dining room is across the entry hall from the kitchen, it gets lovely western light when it receives the most use: in the evening. When I am called upon to remodel a historic house, I have to find ingenious ways to connect the typically separated formal and casual spaces so that a family can live in a more relaxed, modern way. But when I design from scratch, these relationships become easier and more natural—even unconventional—for an architecture of this character.

On the second floor, the compactness of the plan and the central location of the stair hall mean that there are no long hallways needed to connect the three bedrooms—all can be accessed from this central hub. Though I typically like to create buffer zones between public circulation routes and private spaces, that wasn't possible here; instead, I added a column screen at the door to the primary suite, which affords a subtle overlay of what might be described as psychological privacy. Another unusual feature grew out of a memory of my clients' time in England: all the guest rooms are devoid of closets, so visitors must rely on dressers and armoires. While this might seem, in our day and age, a peculiar choice, my clients observe with a wink that it serves to keep guests from overstaying their welcome.

Once again, I am struck by the ways in which designing this house offered so many opportunities to try new things, and the detailing of its interior moldings is just one example. Because of the Grecian connection to English Regency architecture, I researched the work of a British architect named W. F. Pocock, who in 1811 published a pattern book titled *Designs for Rooms*. Like John Soane, a contemporary whose oeuvre is not dissimilar, Pocock took inspiration from the mania for archeology that swept the applied arts in the late eighteenth and early nineteenth centuries; his book features work that reflects not only Grecian precedents, but Egyptian as well. (One finds similar explorations in American architectural pattern books published ten or twenty years later.) Inspired by Pocock's aesthetic inclinations, I was excited to embed, in this relatively restrained setting, moldings and details that answered the aesthetic challenge offered by the sinuous stair and could also subtly link to the Greek Revival spirit that one finds throughout the region. As an architect I am always looking to expand my command of the language of design but also to create a subtext in each of the houses that speaks to its individual sense of place.

As I mentioned earlier, this was meant to be an empty-nester retreat, but with the couple's grown son living one town away, these days the old-fashioned English doorbell is frequently signaling the arrival of grandchildren. It brings me so much joy to see a house for two turned into a place for family gatherings—and to know that the kids are dropping in not just for pizza, but to explore the mysteries of this special place.

OPPOSITE: The stone fireplace mantel, custom crafted in England for the room, draws on Regency precedent and connects to the entirety of the house's molding program.

ABOVE AND OPPOSITE: The paneled library, off the living room, is the couple's preferred cozy retreat; the room opens directly onto the garden as well as the kitchen, an unusual relationship for this kind of house but reflective of modern modes of living. The room's ceiling rosette, based on a Greek Revival precedent, was sculpted by the plaster craftsman David Flaherty.

PREVIOUS PAGES: The laylight's Greek key fretwork serves as an artful air-conditioning grille; the molding designs and column capitals reflect English Regency's Grecian influences (left). The column screen marks the entry to the second-floor primary suite (right). OPPOSITE AND ABOVE: The bathroom in the primary suite forms a bridge between the sleeping quarters and a study.

ABOVE AND OPPOSITE: The kitchen, with its rustic farm table and simple fireplace, makes casual dining especially pleasurable. Uncharacteristically, for this style of residence, the kitchen is just off the front hall, rather than concealed in a separate wing, while the paneled library is just beyond, to the right of the fireplace—another reflection of the way we live today.

LEFT AND ABOVE: The skylit mudroom, with its generously sized soapstone sink for flower cutting and arranging, connects to the pergola and the gardens to the south. (The stair leads to a subterranean gym.)

ABOVE AND RIGHT: The pergola, off the eastern side of the house and overlooking the lower meadows, is a favorite spot for three-season alfresco dining. Behind the high wall topped by lattice-work—an homage to the American classical architect Charles Platt—is the kitchen garden.

PAST PRESENT

Many of my firm's clients envision homes that, to a greater or lesser extent, combine their own present-day realities with their pasts. Sometimes this can be as simple as finding ways to incorporate furnishings or fixtures that belonged to previous generations. Other times we find ourselves renovating family properties, taking care to address new programmatic and aesthetic considerations without erasing beloved architectural touchstones. And now and again—as was the case with this South Florida project—we're called upon to create something new that rests, quite literally, atop a layer of densely textured, and quite significant, personal history.

Yet no matter the circumstances, the fundamental challenge remains precisely the same: How to simultaneously move forward and backward in time? How to blend two very different temporal conditions in a way that lets an individual or a family live life in a modern, joyful way, yet with an awareness of one's personal history—memories which, crucially, must remain a comfort and not a burden? There is never a one-size-fits-all solution: I have discovered, to my continual delight, that everyone's story is unique. And braiding the past and present

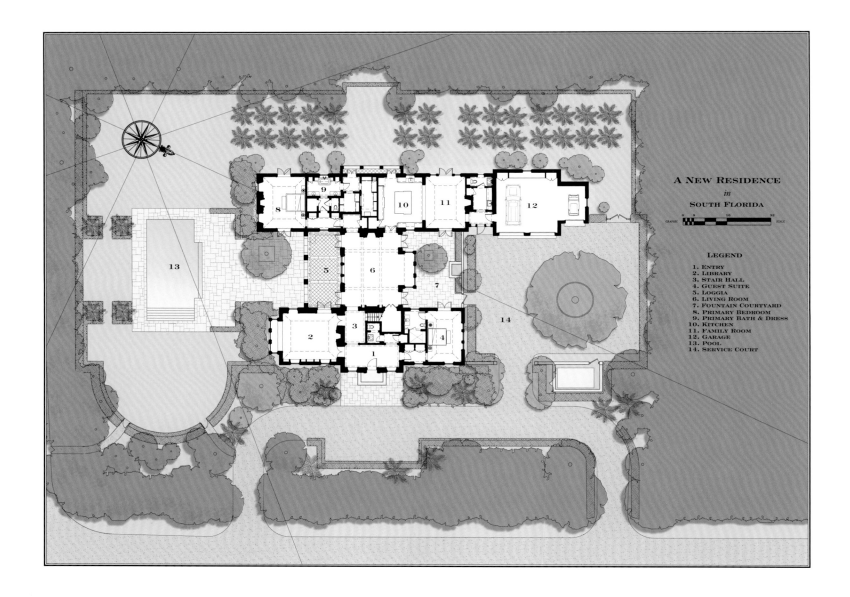

A NEW RESIDENCE
in
SOUTH FLORIDA

GRAPHIC   0 8   16   32   SCALE

LEGEND

1. ENTRY
2. LIBRARY
3. STAIR HALL
4. GUEST SUITE
5. LOGGIA
6. LIVING ROOM
7. FOUNTAIN COURTYARD
8. PRIMARY BEDROOM
9. PRIMARY BATH & DRESS
10. KITCHEN
11. FAMILY ROOM
12. GARAGE
13. POOL
14. SERVICE COURT

in a work of architecture remains, for me, one of the most satisfying of all creative undertakings.

As it happened, I'd worked with these clients before, on a lakeside site in the Adirondacks that was imbued with intergenerational family connections. So it was again with this project: the husband's grandparents had come to this community in the 1940s, and built a house on the then sparsely populated Atlantic seashore. Back in those palmy days, before the area became as popular, and as busy, as it is today, this couple had procured a large piece of property, one that rolled inland for several acres. They eventually downsized to a smaller house away from the water, constructing in 1970 a residence that was

Georgian Caribbean in form and Mediterranean in color palette, containing rooms in which, across many decades, many happy memories were made by four generations.

Initially my team and I were asked to renovate that house, now in the hands of my clients, with the objective of creating

PAGE 92: By setting the house's two-story bar perpendicular—rather than parallel—to the street, we were able to give the entry façade a more modest public profile. PREVIOUS PAGES: The lushly planted entry court. ABOVE: The house's H-shaped floor plan is set within gardens on all four sides. OPPOSITE: The interplay of rooflines, scales, and details—inspired by Anglo-Caribbean precedents—on the animated southern façade.

LEFT: On the house's north side, a low "green wall" separates the parking court from an enclosed garden that sits between two projecting wings—one (at left) containing a guest suite, the other the kitchen and family room.

OPPOSITE AND ABOVE: The house's exterior details particularize the architectural style and shift back and forth between Georgian formality and Anglo-Caribbean vernacular casualness. (Beauty and function go hand in hand: the railing's elegant tracery is also code-compliant.) The blue-green of the shutters and front door serves as an introduction to the residence's interior palette and captures the character of a tropical dwelling.

ABOVE: The stair portal, with an elongated arched architrave molding, reflects the residents' preference for a measure of architectural formality, even in this relaxed setting. OPPOSITE: A view of the entry hall, with its vibrant coral fabrics, turquoise silk wallpaper, and limestone floor, looking toward the library.

a winter retreat for the couple and their three high-school- and college–age daughters—*and* make it a place that would welcome the generations to come. Fitting in the family's program, alas, would have involved all but demolishing the structure, so we suggested starting over. Apart from the impossibility of effectively reconciling what they wanted with what they had, two additional considerations motivated our thinking. The first was that the property, as arranged around the existing building, was underutilized: a new house would enable a more comprehensive, and felicitous, garden-and-landscape experience on all sides of the building. The other consideration had to do with the way in which the structure presented itself to the street. This community is unusual in the sense that, while there are no stylistic restrictions on what you can build, imposing your home on your neighbors is considered most unwelcome—the idea is, do what you wish, but keep it to yourself (a philosophy as sound in architecture as it is in life). I knew that a more private relationship to the street could be developed via the right sort of buffer planting. But I also felt that the house, if properly designed, could present itself at once more elegantly and discreetly.

Our clients came to agree. But, quite apart from their wish to preserve the emotional history of the generations that had visited the original house—the accretion of intimate moments that, bit by bit, had created a prismatic, panoramic personal legacy—they also understood the particular character of the community and how its habits and traditions had infiltrated local domestic life. The spirit of the area was a significant component of their memory, and it was essential for my office to preserve that as well.

LEFT: A Chinese jar exuberantly filled with palm fronds, set on a long table, separates back-to-back sofas in the living room. Each serves a different sitting area: one focused on the fireplace, the other facing the television. The formal dining table occupies a bay overlooking the enclosed courtyard garden on the house's north side.

ABOVE: I particularly enjoy the pairing of the traditional moldings, mantelpiece, and beamwork with the brightly colored walls, given a crosshatch glaze by the talented decorative painter Agustin Hurtado. OPPOSITE: A view toward the entry hall. The tall, elegant built-in Georgian-style cabinet to the left of the doorway, which we designed for the room, conceals a television.

Knowing that the house would have a substantial number of requirements, my first consideration was how to fit everything elegantly onto the site, while also making the structure visually modest. The solution—abetted by the generous size of the lot, which afforded us an extra measure of creative flexibility—was an H-shaped plan. The two-story "crossbar" of the H is set perpendicular to the street, so that when you drive past—or even when you pull up to the front of the house—you don't really perceive it. Rather, you're greeted by an understated front door, set into a low-key façade. The place doesn't even seem particularly big when you walk into the entry hall: you see, to your left, a cypress-paneled library, and a guest suite to your right. It's not until you begin venturing deeper into the house—passing through the stair hall and into the generous living/dining room that consumes the entirety of the H's crossbar, and continuing on to the house's rear, with the adjoining kitchen and family room to one side, and the primary bedroom suite on the other—that the scale of the house begins to reveal itself. And when you mount the stairs to the upper level of the crossbar, you discover—off a long hallway that opens onto a graciously scaled deck—three full bedroom-and-bath suites. Only then do you realize you are in a two-story, five-bedroom house disguised as a pastel-colored Anglo-Caribbean beach cottage.

An H plan offers other advantages, too: Many of the rooms have windows and/or French doors on three sides (indeed, the primary suite seems to reside in its own private pavilion), and the axes and cross-axes enable views across exterior spaces into the rooms beyond, a rich layering and interplay of indoor and outdoor experience that gives the

RIGHT: The library occupies the precise spot in the plan that its much-beloved predecessor held within the owner's previous house and is paneled in much of that room's original cypress. The room resides in its own pavilion off the entry hall and has windows on three sides.

house an overlay of complexity and charm. And because the structure is only one room wide at its center, I was able to insert a loggia overlooking the pool and lawn on one side of the living/dining space and a private enclosed courtyard with a fountain on its other side. An H plan isn't always an option, of course. But when possible, it opens the way to a very special kind of experiential richness, letting every room engage in some way with both natural light and the landscape, while encouraging a heightened appreciation of the particular character of the architecture.

I also gave careful consideration to the house's style, crafting a profile that was elegantly at home amongst its neighbors without being precisely at one with them. In my experience, there is a broad stylistic lexicon to draw on in South Florida, ranging from low-slung and ranch-like to Mizner Mediterranean and Bermudian or Caribbean Georgian. My clients, though relaxed, fun-loving individuals, nevertheless like a certain formality in their houses. What I landed on, in the end, was something in the middle, an architectural vocabulary with Georgian proportions and details, yet more at ease—you'll find rafter tails at the roof line rather than a box cornice, and cedar shakes on the roof. The outcome is relaxed without being raffish, tailored but not overbearing. And the overall effect is nicely enlivened by the color palette in the interior, which my team and I helped to decorate with the wife. My clients are notably cheerful people, and embrace the joyful character of tropical hues—bright greens and yellows, as well as blue/turquoise and salmon/coral, which we interwove and carried through the house within and without. Finding precisely the right balance of elements—architectural, decorative, historical, nostalgic— is an undertaking that I always relish. Making homes that families can enjoy today, tomorrow, and beyond is both a pleasure and energizing. The more I do it, the more I learn, and the greater the satisfaction.

Not the least of the fun derives from collaboration, in this case with the resourceful and intuitive Chilean landscape designer Cecilia de Grelle. Like myself, Cecilia sought to extract the maximum from the property's potential while serving memory and history. On its southern side, the old house had a pool set in a big open lawn where the younger generations had happily run around and tossed lacrosse balls, and this one does, too. But we both knew that the patch of garden along the property's western edge, which in its old iteration had been a forlorn area reserved for yard clippings and noisy air-conditioning compressors, was now an important space with a necklace of rooms that opened onto it, including the primary suite, the kitchen, and the family room. Cecilia's insertion of a palm allée transforms that narrow strip of land into something visually exciting and experientially meaningful—another place to walk in the garden or set a long table for lunch

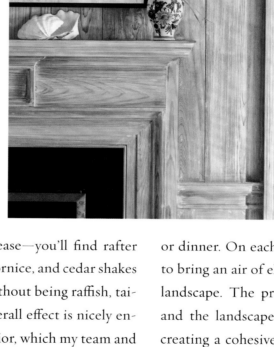

or dinner. On each of the house's four sides, Cecilia was able to bring an air of elegance, utility, and sense of purpose to the landscape. The property is used well and comprehensively, and the landscape supports and enhances the architecture, creating a cohesive experience that helps make the home an exceptionally satisfying place to be.

ABOVE: The library combines the cypress paneling from the original room with our newly crafted elements, including the mantelpiece, wainscoting, and door surround (also cypress). OPPOSITE: The kitchen opens out to the new garden on the house's western side. To the right of the marble-topped kitchen island is the family room.

ABOVE AND OPPOSITE: In collaboration with the project's imaginative landscape designer, Cecilia de Grelle, we created a spectacular palm allée in the property's westernmost precinct, an area that was previously an unloved afterthought. French doors from the family room lead out to a table set for lunch.

ABOVE AND OPPOSITE: One of the benefits of an H-shaped plan is that it creates open spaces between the house's projecting wings—for example, this loggia overlooking the pool, which is set between the pavilions containing the library and primary suite (with the living room at the rear) and fully furnished for living, dining, and game-playing. Motorized screens, concealed in the arches, can be lowered to keep the bugs out.

PREVIOUS PAGES: On the opposite side of the house from the pool, there is a garden overlooked by the living room's dining bay. It is accessed from the living room, as well as from a guest suite on one side and the family room on the other. The fountain, set into the wall that separates the garden from the parking court, creates a soothing sound that increases the sense of privacy and peace. ABOVE AND OPPOSITE: The primary suite, at once formal and serene, occupies its own wing at the back of the residence and benefits from glazing on three sides. The tray ceiling gives the bedroom a lofty air; the oversized soaking tub in the bath overlooking the garden on the house's western side supports the sense of relaxation and retreat that pervades the entirety of the pavilion.

OPPOSITE: In the upstairs hallway, the detailing of the ceiling suggests that the space might once have been an open porch. (In fact, there is a terrace beyond the glass doors at left that overlooks the pool.) ABOVE: In addition to offering an abundance of closet space, the hall connects to three tray-ceilinged bedroom suites, including this one.

I have mentioned the idea of personal history as a comfort rather than a burden. The house accomplishes this in two ways. One is through the reuse of decorative and utilitarian elements from the previous residence, such as the original brass door hardware, as well as some of the fireplace mantels; this approach helps to awaken, not only visual memory, but also the tactile experience embedded in one's subconscious. The sense of the past is conveyed through touch. But the most significant gesture to what had been before is the library. In the old house, this cypress-paneled room was the one in which memories were made, at get-togethers, on holidays and during special occasions. To enable the family to continue that tradition, we effectively recreated the room reusing the original cypress boards, replicating the spatial dimensions, and putting it in the same place in the plan. I can't think of a more meaningful way to make history new— or to make new history.

Houses aren't always subjected to what might be described as an acid test, but this one was, most assuredly: during Covid, the entire family checked in for an extended live-work cohabitation that included the three daughters and some of their significant others. That's a lot of adults under one roof for a considerable duration—not something that always goes well. Yet everyone managed to stake out a corner in which to be happily, productively alone, while also enjoying the particular satisfactions of being together. Probably no one anticipated making those kinds of memories. But now they have, and that moment of family history has joined the long march of time on this land—one that will continue, to be sure, for generations to come.

RIGHT: The view across the pool reveals the terrace between the library and primary suite pavilions and, just beyond through the archways, the loggia off the living room. The long terrace on the second floor can be accessed from the upstairs hallway. FOLLOWING PAGES: Paradise at sunset.

DOUBLING DOWN (EAST)

As a practitioner specializing in residential architecture, I devote considerable time and imagination to devising houses that can accommodate, and be enjoyed by, families. Many of my clients, in the fullness of their maturity, build homes precisely because they want to be surrounded by their loved ones and come to our office for what I often refer to as "grandchildren magnets": houses designed specifically to appeal to, and attract, the focus, energies, and imagination of a family's younger generations.

So it was slightly unusual when a couple asked me to do the exact opposite: to create a residential experience that, while enabling people (kin and otherwise) to visit, ensured their privacy and autonomy and kept virtually everything (and everyone) else at a friendly but distinct distance: to, in effect, split the program between *us* and *them*. And while the assignment was initially surprising, in the end it allowed us to create something truly unique and special. With apologies to Abraham Lincoln: Sometimes a house divided actually *can* stand.

The clients in question wished to build a one-bedroom residence on a sublime, semi-secluded point of land, one that extended into the harbor at the southern end of a bay in a classic "Down East" Maine town. Though they expected to entertain, the program the couple envisioned would largely exclude the usual complement of extra rooms, instead focusing on the way they liked to spend time together, just the two of them. All other aspects of their household—not only guest accommodations, but a gym, a garage, and laundry, storage, and support spaces—were to be located on a separate piece of property a short stroll away. As a result, my clients wouldn't need to overload their waterside idyll with an excess of rooms, thereby obscuring the open vistas afforded by their special circumstances. And while there would be architectural similarities between the two properties, these, it was imagined, would be not so much nominal as subliminal, with the house on the point remaining a stylistic descendant of its turn-of-the-last-century predecessors, and the inland "support" structure emerging as . . . something else.

We undertook the design of the primary, waterside residence first. Though I didn't want the layout to be bilaterally symmetrical but rather to feel like a place that had been added onto over time, the plan that emerged did indeed have two wings. One featured the kitchen and dining porch, butler's pantry/bar, den, and mudroom, while the other contained the private quarters, with an expansive living room occupying the zone between them. Simple enough—but there were nevertheless unusual architectural challenges.

In this book's introduction, I cited Thomas Hastings's very useful maxim, "Style is the problem solved." But what happens when the problem to be solved is stylistic? It is not

PAGE 126: The house's entry façade. What appears to be a partial second story is in fact unoccupied: an architectural artifice designed to prevent a dwelling on the Maine coast from looking like a one-story California ranch house.
PREVIOUS PAGES: The house commands a point extending into one of Down East Maine's most picturesque harbors.
RIGHT: The formal entry porch has a modest cousin: an inset side door that leads to the house's mudroom.

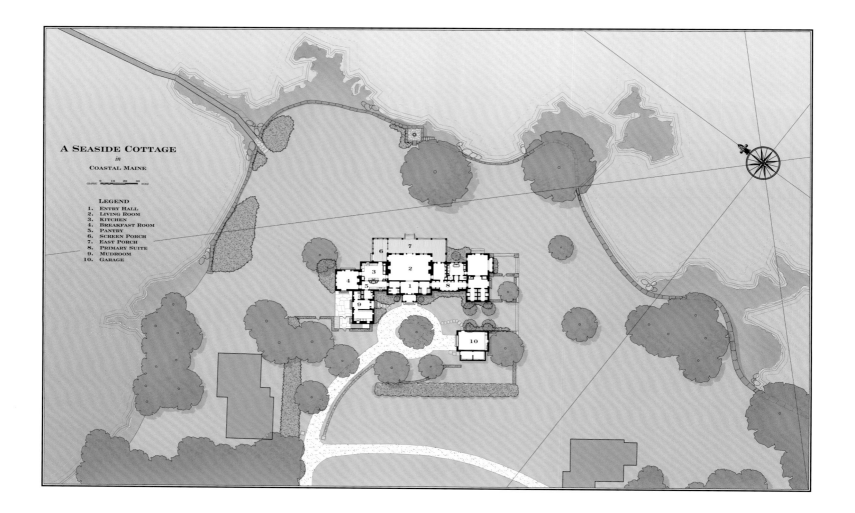

A SEASIDE COTTAGE
in
COASTAL MAINE

LEGEND
1. ENTRY HALL
2. LIVING ROOM
3. KITCHEN
4. BREAKFAST ROOM
5. PANTRY
6. SCREEN PORCH
7. EAST PORCH
8. PRIMARY SUITE
9. MUDROOM
10. GARAGE

so easy, I discovered, to design a single-story, single-bedroom dwelling that's bigger than a cottage but smaller than a rambling grand manse. What appears on the drawing board is effectively a ranch house—which is utterly out of character for coastal Maine. The abundant local historic precedents were at least a story and a half, with picturesque bump-outs extending off the main volume. Thus my challenge: how to design a de facto "rancher" that looked like what a Maine dwelling is supposed to look like?

The solution was to make the middle of the house taller, so that from the outside there appears to be a partial second story. To do so, we added front and back cross gables, on the north and south elevations, with windows that light attic space on one side and draw down sunlight into the living room on the other—in effect, an architectural ruse. This gambit did the trick: The resulting house, rather than resembling something better suited to Southern California, looks entire-

ly appropriate to the coast of Maine, an impression reinforced by the pleasing asymmetrical irregularities produced by the dining porch, primary suite, and mudroom.

That was one challenge. Then there was another. My clients had lived for a time in France, where they had collected handsome continental antique furniture that they wanted to bring to their new home. Here again was a stylistic conundrum, as Flemish, French, and Italian furniture seemed to me to be aesthetically at odds with a shingle-clad house on the Maine waterfront. Typically, in our practice, architecture precedes decoration, but in this case—at least on the inside—it

ABOVE: The floor plan reveals the house's many opportunities for water views afforded by the property's dramatic shape and position. OPPOSITE: The entry porch's pergola, with its latticework insets that play host to climbing roses, frames a view through the foyer and living room to the harbor beyond.

ABOVE AND OPPOSITE: The foyer, which connects to the living room, features a compendium of nineteenth-century Down East Maine's classic architectural components: sidelights, a transom, and the upper part of a Dutch door, all with diamond-pane windows; vertical paneling on the walls; and a bowed ceiling reminiscent of that of a sailboat cabin. The laylight in the ceiling brings in natural illumination captured by the gable windows above.

was a matter of *cherchez la furniture*. How to add a European overlay to the architecture that would welcome the couple's collection without clashing with the house's overall aesthetic?

I began by firmly establishing the regional character of the architecture in the house's entry. A very wide Dutch door is flanked by diamond-pane sidelights—both typical, and much beloved, features of Maine summer residences. Once inside, in a vestibule more generously proportioned than is usual, I further localized the experience with what is known as a laylight: a flat piece of glass in the ceiling that captures the sunlight from the windows in the cross gable above it and acts as a skylight, of the sort sometimes found on sailing vessels. This nautical motif is reinforced by a gently vaulted ceiling that recalls the header of a below-deck cabin in a sailboat; beadboard walls, a common feature of Maine houses from the turn of the last century, further anchor the aesthetic in Down East traditions.

The entry opens directly into the living room, via a broad doorway topped by a transom, and here the architecture shades into something more compatible with my clients' furniture. The room, with its soaring ceiling, is a full one and a half stories in height, and while the sawn timbers in its upper register might be found holding up the roof of a New England barn, their more formal character suggests a French country house or chateau. We also surfaced the walls in a semi-smooth hand-troweled Belgian plaster to create a very different, distinctly continental feeling from the beadboard in the entry; handsome twin stone mantelpieces at each end of the room, custom crafted in England, ground the space in a quiet sophistication (and provide elegant underpinnings for the Dutch mirrors suspended above each). My clients' *objets* seem entirely at home in this environment—and the subtle blending of small-town Maine and rural France feels surprisingly natural and pleasing.

RIGHT: The living room artfully blends elements evocative of French country châteaux and Maine coastal dwellings, the better to accommodate my clients' collection of antique continental furniture. Troweled plaster walls and oak trusses suggest a predominant European influence.

Two of my obsessions, as an architect, are views and light, and the waterfront site (with its multiple exposures), and the fact that the usual concessions to privacy weren't necessary, presented multiple opportunities to maximize both. The house is an essay in the satisfactions of axiality: stepping into the hallway between the entry and living room, looking left and right, one beholds the residence from end to end, and the slenderness of the structure enables multiple cross-axes, so that even on overcast days the sun's transit is felt from all directions, and the eye is met by boats bobbing in the chop, the mountains to the north, the buzz of the harbor, and the open sea. The main enfilade also afforded the opportunity to give this book-loving couple a combination hallway/library in the English style: a place to pause, take down a volume, recline on the window seat, and enjoy an absorbing read.

There's a lot to be said for having a house for two. There are doors, but you don't usually need them, so that the architecture, for all of its presence, feels almost evanescent. Conversely, your awareness of your surroundings is heightened, as at any given moment you can see so much of it. The sense of being at home is something we all cherish, and how sweet it is, for this couple, to experience that feeling with such resonance and depth. Yet as successfully self-contained as the primary residence is, it still needed the other part—the guesthouse—to complete the experience. Fortuitously, my clients were able to secure another property located just a short walk from the main house. Yet the settings and circumstances were so different—and, to me, so initially daunting—that an entirely different set of responses was needed to make it all work.

Whereas the house on the point benefitted from the in-built beauty and drama of its waterside circumstances, the sloping acre my clients had procured for the inland guest compound, a mere block away, was an empty piece of sloping land—virtually a field, on a nondescript street with suburban houses on either side and behind it. It was not only unsightly and unpromising, but the very opposite of what you'd expect to find in the bucolic, sea-scented precincts of coastal Maine.

Even before I had an architectural idea, it was evident that our first task would be to cancel out the surroundings, and create a place that would be a world unto itself.

This thought was rapidly followed by a question: What sort of narrative could I devise that might unite, not only two different buildings, but two such different properties? Pondering the possibilities, I stepped back, in my mind, to the region around the harbor, and realized that the area was rich in small family compounds—what were sometimes called, in a less enlightened age, "gentlemen's farms"—from the turn of the last century. These were often comprised of comfortable houses (cousins to the one on the point) in close proximity to working barns surrounding enclosed pastures. This presented a promising opportunity: I could conceive of the suburban lot as the main house's farm compound, a trio of vernacular-style structures overlooking a central courtyard, further cushioned by an outer layer of landscape that screened off the adjacent properties. The sloped site was our ally in this regard, as it created the opportunity for a "bank barn," a structure that is partly embedded in a hillside: you go in the front door on the first floor, up some stairs, and walk out the back on the second—in both cases with your feet on the ground.

The site plan I had in mind was simple, a U-shaped arrangement comprised of three buildings: the barn-style guest residence at the bottom of the U, with a garage/bike shed on one side, and a cutting garden and gym/garden shed on the other, all looking onto a center courtyard filled with fruit trees—what one local, upon seeing the finished product, wittily characterized as a "farmlet." To realize this vision, however, I needed an imaginative and resourceful collaborator, and I was immensely fortunate to find myself working—on both properties—with landscape architect Stephen Mohr and

OPPOSITE: The living room's twin mantelpieces, with their distinctive pulvinated friezes, set at each end of the room, were made in England from fossil stone found in Dorset. At this end, the space opens to a small study. Transoms, used throughout, increase the sense of connectivity between rooms.

PREVIOUS PAGES: A detail of the ceiling truss; a hallway-cum-library with a cozy window seat for reading; one of the mantelpieces; a powder room off the foyer (*left, clockwise from upper left*). A dormer in the faux second story brings light into the great room (*right*). LEFT AND ABOVE: Knotty-pine paneling adds unfussy warmth to a cozy den and dining room at the house's north end.

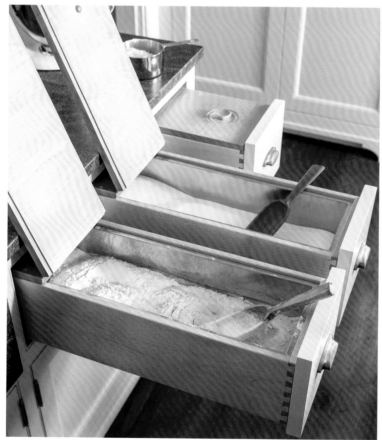

PREVIOUS PAGES: For a couple that loves to cook and bake, we crafted a kitchen that enables them to each pursue their particular culinary passions, taking care to ensure that both tools and ingredients are always conveniently at hand. ABOVE AND OPPOSITE: The sole bedroom/bathroom suite, at the house's southern end, enjoys harbor and bay views.

PAGES 148-9: The mudroom features two doors: one from the motor court (left) and the other, on the room's opposite side, leading out to a terrace overlooking the harbor (right). PREVIOUS PAGES: The house's north end, with its waterside screen porch and the layered gables that give the simple structure an overlay of architectural complexity and visual interest. RIGHT: On the dining porch, the screens can be replaced with glass panels when the bugs depart and the chilly weather arrives. (Heating elements in the ceiling boost the warmth as needed.)

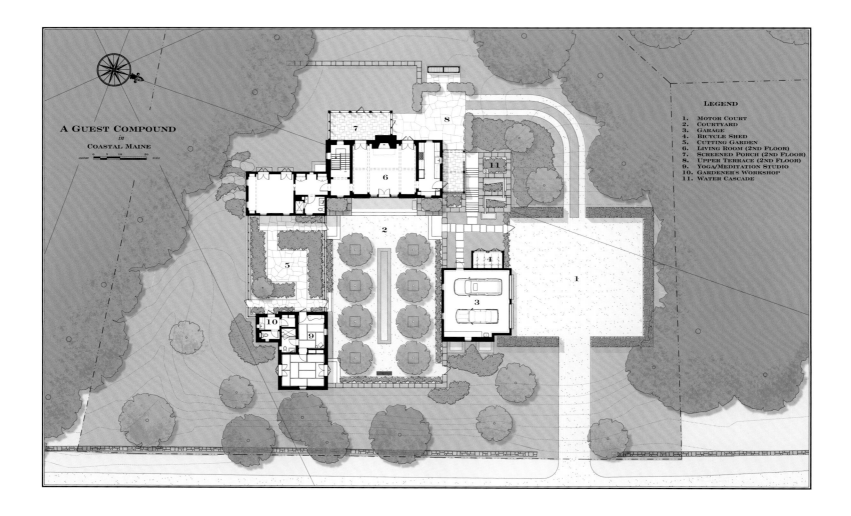

A GUEST COMPOUND
in
COASTAL MAINE

his partner, Tatyanna Seredin. Their distinct visions sensitively captured, and enhanced, the virtues of each location.

During the project, our clients journeyed to Japan, and while their enthusiasm for what they discovered would touch every aspect of this project, the pictures they showed Stephen and me of gardens and buildings there—combined with the abundance of Maine granite available to us—impacted our approach to the design of the guest compound most dramatically. It inspired us to shape a long, trough-like water feature flanked by rows of apple trees in the guest compound's courtyard (which Stephen enclosed, on the side overlooking the street, with a low wall of the same irregularly cut stone), and a sublimely rendered water cascade, flowing down past an exterior stone stair that leads to the slope-top behind the house. Using our conceptual drawings as a starting place, Stephen also added an outer layer of mature vegetation, which makes the space feel as though it's nestled in the woods, rather than

the suburbs. Once the ensemble—architecture, gardens, landscape—was complete, the outcome was startling: an enclave unmistakably Japanese in its conception and execution, yet perfectly in keeping with the region's agricultural roots.

Different factors and influences impacted the design of the compound's residential component. When a building is partly embedded in the earth, the section below ground must be masonry clad to hold back the dirt and moisture; this necessity inspired us to construct the courtyard-facing lower floor from the same rough-hewn granite as its surroundings,

ABOVE AND OPPOSITE: At the heart of the guest compound, conceived with a distinctly different character than the main house, a long stone trough, flanked by apple trees, suggests the agrarian influence underpinning the design. The arrangement, which draws on the region's farmsteads, also taps into Japanese precedents.
FOLLOWING PAGES: A view of the compound from the street. A stone wall and more apple trees add a layer of privacy.

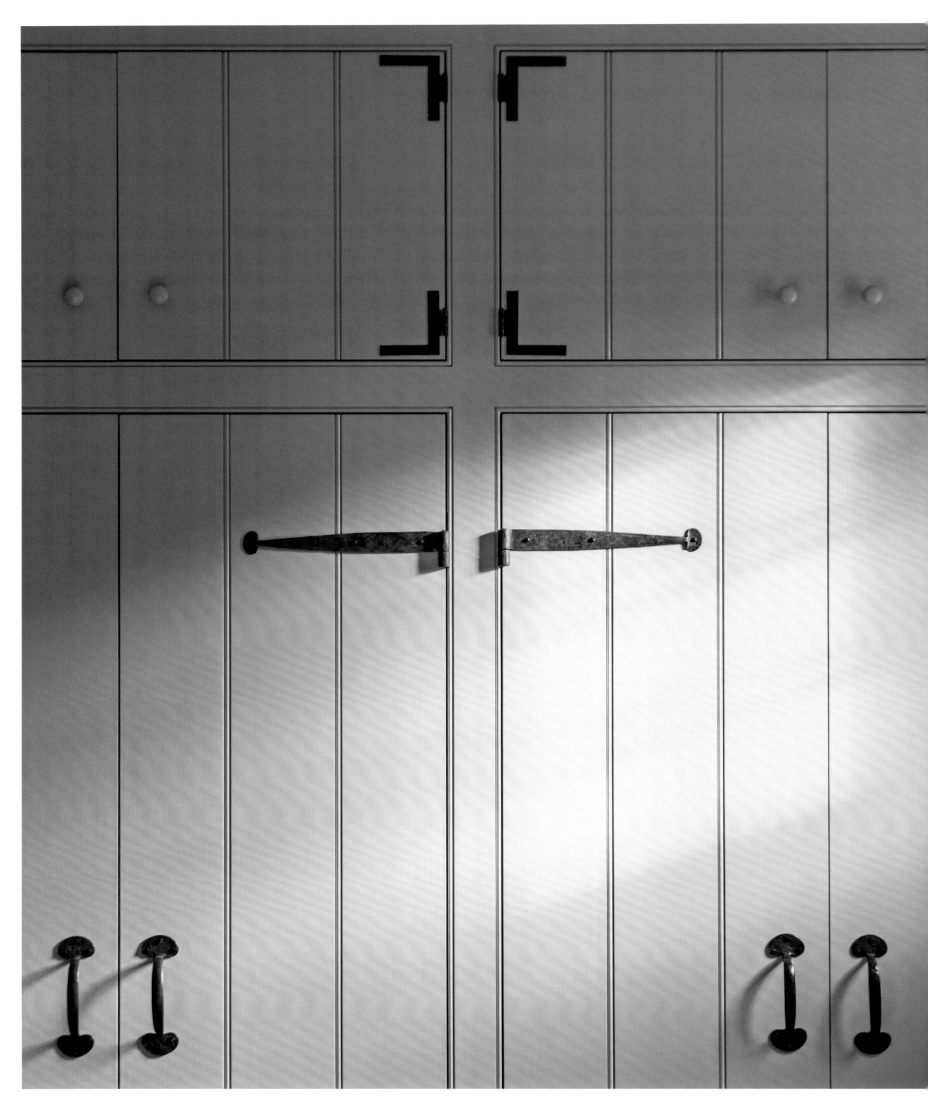

PAGES 158-9: Details of the courtyard, and a view of the bank barn–style guest cottage from the motor court. PREVIOUS PAGES: The glazed entry hall, with its barn wood siding and beams, utilitarian lanterns, and Japanese screen, is the house's most Asian moment, yet the local traditions persist (Shaker bench and wrought-iron hardware among them). OPPOSITE AND ABOVE: On the bank barn's second floor, the great room with its rough-hewn beams, barn wood siding, and rustic stone chimney breast. Our builder's accomplished craftspeople infused the architecture with hands-on authenticity.

ABOVE AND OPPOSITE: The visual relationship between the great room's monolithic hearthstone and the artwork, by Julian Meredith, wasn't intentional, but it is startling and appealing. The mix of American, English, and continental furnishings is similar to that in the main house, but more relaxed.

producing a welcome cohesiveness. Into this façade we set three barn-sized glazed French doors that serve as entry portals (and find an echo directly above, in sliding panels on the second story), to suggest a farm building that has been converted to a garden pavilion. Entering the long vestibule that connects to a downstairs bedroom suite, as well as storage and utility rooms, one finds a space in which Asian and American strands overlap and intersect: a painted screen decorated with floral and garden motifs, discovered by my clients on their Japan trip, hangs above a quietly bravura contemporary Shaker-style bench in black walnut. The reclaimed barn siding on the walls and ceiling, industrial metal pendant lights, and flagstone floor contribute to a mood that—like so many aspects of this project—seems at once both local and global.

Upstairs, we restated the motifs deployed so elegantly in the primary residence in a more rustic language: rather than a classically inspired mantelpiece, the living room fireplace is framed by rugged granite blocks, the most astonishing of which is the enormous hearthstone, which seems to have emerged directly out of the earth. The chateau-style beam work of the main house is here exchanged for a rough-hewn barn-style superstructure supporting the peaked ceiling, set against rough boards rather than Belgian plaster (though that material appears in the bedrooms). The one constant is the continental character of the furnishings—though what reads as sophisticated on the point seems farmhouse-appropriate in this environment. Let me add that none of this, in either locale, would be possible without the exceptional craft tradition that exists in Maine. Though Jay Fischer, the phenomenal contractor who built both houses, was armed with sheets and sheets of our drawings, he also knows intuitively how to produce work of the very highest quality. Just as the decorative element plays an ever more important role in our architectural thinking, so, too, do the hands of the contractor and landscaper. It is all of us working together, in pursuit of a client's vision, that transforms any project—and perhaps this one in particular—into a work both complete and cohesive.

And speaking of that client vision: what I had originally foreseen as a combination gym and garden shed on the south side of the courtyard received its own unexpected artistic transformation over the course of the project, into a temple-inspired meditation and yoga pavilion. Upon their return from that trip to Asia, midway through design development, the couple expressed astonishment (and disappointment) that I had never visited Japan and experienced the architecture and gardens there in three dimensions. Thus shamed, I voyaged to Kyoto and, like so many of my predecessors, returned with transformed sensibilities. What I saw guided me, with their encouragement, to rethink the interior of that shed into a miniature teahouse, a quiet world of tatami mats and upholstered linen walls, live-edge wood and fabric shades, embodying the cross-cultural perspectives of Isamu Noguchi and George Nakashima. The environment is pristine, precise, and peaceful: ideally suited to the very practices my clients pursue within it.

This last experience suggests one of the great personal benefits of this unusual project in particular, and the pursuit of architecture in general: I am always learning. To learn requires not only the confidence, faith, and humility that come with experience, but a willingness to be open to suggestions and then to do the hard work required to achieve them. For all of this, I am most grateful for the clients who've pushed me into places I might never have gone on my own. Over the years I have come to understand that this is the path to becoming a better practitioner—and it's a good rule of thumb for life, too.

OPPOSITE: A small screened porch, off the living room on the second floor, overlooks the upper garden and gathers evening light.

ABOVE AND OPPOSITE: The upstairs bedroom, with its lime-washed beams, refined plasterwork, and antique furniture, reflects the project's mix of elegance and rusticity.

RIGHT AND OPPOSITE: The guest cottage was meant to relieve the main house of utilitarian burdens; here you will find spaces devoted to laundry, storage, gardening, and other functions—no less handsome for being "back of house."

ABOVE, OPPOSITE, AND FOLLOWING PAGES: On the far side of the courtyard, what was originally meant to be a garden shed has now become a yoga/meditation/exercise pavilion heavily influenced by the design of teahouses in Kyoto. The tatami mats were crafted in Japan specifically to fit the spaces.

A SINGULAR SENSIBILITY

I'm probably not your typical "classical" architect. Perhaps because my education included a healthy dose of modernism along with all the history I took in, I've never viewed classicism as a strict discipline with rigid boundaries. Instead, I have always regarded it as a vibrant, living language that allows its practitioners to speak it in fluid and inventive ways—making it equally relevant to the present age as it was to the past. This doesn't mean that I like to play fast and loose with the style; it just means, to me at least, that classicism can be applied to any number of architectural problems with as much facility as a more contemporary design idiom.

Why? Well, unlike many architectural genres that have their roots in history, classicism is particularly elastic—a multitude of practitioners in the residential realm, from Robert Adam to Edwin Lutyens to David Adler, have pushed and pulled it in numerous imaginative directions—and it can also be a surprisingly agreeable partner to seemingly unrelated styles. I have discovered over the last twenty years that the pursuit of classical, as well as traditional vernacular, architecture has enabled me to work with any number of clients on projects that defy any number of expectations. This house—*ensemble* is perhaps a more accurate word—is a wonderful example.

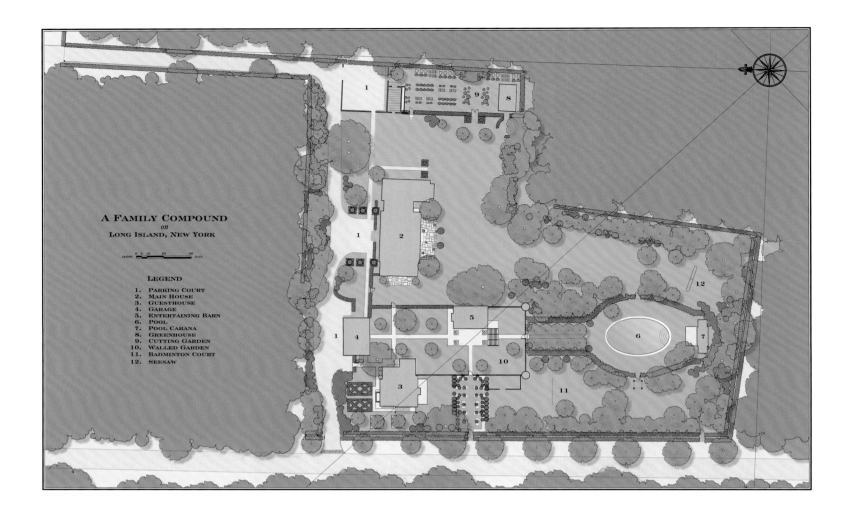

A FAMILY COMPOUND
on
LONG ISLAND, NEW YORK

LEGEND

1. PARKING COURT
2. MAIN HOUSE
3. GUESTHOUSE
4. GARAGE
5. ENTERTAINING BARN
6. POOL
7. POOL CABANA
8. GREENHOUSE
9. CUTTING GARDEN
10. WALLED GARDEN
11. BADMINTON COURT
12. SEESAW

The couple that engaged me to design this eastern Long Island compound hail from two very different locales with vastly different cultures—Colombia and Connecticut—fused into a single, and singular, sensibility. The outcome of this alchemy is a refined and sophisticated international aesthetic, one that embraces (on an equal footing) fashion, music, fine art, design of every sort, and craft. If there is a single overriding characteristic, it is a severe allergy to the expected. Separately and together, these two never want to do the obvious, and so it was with the residence they decided to build for themselves and their two young children.

Though the project was commissioned for a region known for the enormity of its mansions—and McMansions, typically in one or another variant of the Shingle Style—the wife had no interest in engaging in the look-how-big-our-house-is game. Rather, she wanted a less imposing residence—a house rather than a colossus—and one in the Colo-

nial Revival style that she'd grown up with in the leafy environs of Connecticut. But the pair did have a substantial program, and both wanted to incorporate a variety of ways to entertain, in a range of settings, and at different scales, always with their signature generosity of spirit at the center. Thus they asked me to divide up the functions that might, under other circumstances, reside under one roof, and effectively scatter them across the property, as though they were follies integrated into a garden.

The couple gave me the perfect partner for this assignment: Miranda Brooks, an always inventive landscape designer

PAGE 176: Connecticut comes to eastern Long Island: a view of the Colonial Revival–style main house as seen from its entry court. ABOVE: This family compound accommodates a broad range of buildings, gardens, influences, and moods. OPPOSITE: The primary structure's south façade, overlooking an expanse of broad lawn.

LEFT: The bones of the entry hall are Federal and Colonial Revival classicism, as reflected in the archway, paneling, and stair details. These serve as the ground of a colorful, eclectic—indeed, freewheeling—palette of art and decoration, including a stair runner inspired by midcentury Swedish carpets.

RIGHT: A view from the entry hall, through a portal edged with exceptionally refined classical moldings, into the library, which mixes lime-washed pine millwork with bookcases and walls upholstered in hand-blocked batik fabric. Contemporary art and Scandinavian furniture from the twentieth century pair comfortably with expressive wainscoting and a reclaimed wide-plank pine floor.

RIGHT: The living room runs the full width of the center block of the house; the ceiling is set slightly lower than one might expect in a room of this scale, to suggest that the vast space might once have been two separate rooms separated by a center hall. Windows along one side of the room overlook the property's main lawn and pocket up into the wall above them when open; a glazed porch is accessed via the doors flanking the fireplace (one of two in the room). The boldly graphic rug was designed for the setting.

PREVIOUS PAGES: Two ends of the glazed porch, which incorporates a well-curated potpourri of architectural elements and furniture pieces, among them a column screen and decorative stone floor, a Giacometti-style table, and wicker chairs. The room's exuberant antique stone mantel was found for the owners by interior designer David Netto, who also decorated the property's guest cottage. OPPOSITE AND ABOVE: The tone changes in the informal rooms at the house's north end, notably in the well-equipped mudroom, reached via a back door. Rustic ceiling beams, beadboard paneling, and a reclaimed cathedral-stone floor establish the informal mood.

PREVIOUS PAGES: A flower sink is conveniently located adjacent to the mudroom and just inside the house's back door, which leads to a nearby cutting garden (*left*). In the butler's pantry, a custom-designed china cabinet holds the bounty of a couple who enjoy cooking and entertaining in equal measure (*right*). OPPOSITE AND ABOVE: Two views of the kitchen, with its immense Italian stove and plasterwork range hood, rough-hewn ceiling beams, and banquette and breakfast table overlooking the garden.

OPPOSITE AND ABOVE: My clients' bold embrace of pattern and color is on display once again in the primary bedroom suite. The walls are upholstered in an embroidered fabric; a classic twentieth-century artwork hangs above the simple yet elegant Federal-style mantelpiece that we custom designed for the room.

RIGHT AND FOLLOWING PAGES: The lady's bath and dressing room, which extends its utility via the inclusion of a daybed and writing desk, combines a multitude of influences: the closets, with their drapery under glass, draw on French precedents; the decorative tiles in the fireplace are Dutch; and the floating tub and a sink perched between windows are English country-house gestures. The "closet" closest to the fireplace hides the shower.

with a predilection for the unpretentious and naturalistic. Our canvas? Two adjoining properties, combined into a single L-shaped lot. Working together, Miranda and I set about the tricky enterprise of roughing out a site plan, determining where the main house and its outbuilding structures would go and how the various garden elements might create relationships between them. This was crucial, not only to maximize the project's experiential variety, but because each architectural element would be paired with one or more corresponding landscape moments. Once we arrived at a plan—in close collaboration with our clients, especially when it came to developing opportunities for outdoor entertaining—I was able to turn my attention to the buildings.

One of the two properties that my clients combined featured a nineteenth-century farmhouse and a late twentieth-century garage in the site's northwestern quadrant, and that is where the architecture commenced: the farmhouse was reimagined and renovated to become a three-bedroom guesthouse, and the garage was taken down to its foundation and resurrected as an entertaining barn, with a robust outdoor kitchen and a dining pergola. The new barn features big pocketing glass doors on its east and west sides that, when pushed open, transform the building into a portal between the two sides of the landscape. Completing the architectural ensemble is a new garage, also carefully positioned so that one side opens, appropriately, onto the property's driveway, while the other connects to a walled garden shared by the guesthouse and barn. Should my clients so choose, they can open the garden-facing doors of the structure, and transform it into a drinks pavilion—providing this delightfully sociable couple

with yet another way to entertain. As for that walled garden, it too is multivalent: incorporating tree-shaded sitting and lounging areas, the barn's outdoor kitchen and dining pergola, and, at the corners of its southern wall, a pair of tiny cylindrical pavilions—one for storing badminton racquets, the other slyly concealing a pizza oven.

A gate in that southern wall connects to one of Miranda's more magical creations, an allée flanked by sycamore trees that leads to the oval-shaped swimming pool. (Great lovers of alfresco dining, my clients also use the allée for lunches and dinners.) On the far side of that pool, we set a cabana structure conceived as an architectural folly, one that encapsulates the enchantments of the Long Island summer: fashioned from metal and painted with green and white stripes, it has the look of a whimsical tented pavilion. Call it Charlottenburg Palace, by way of Palm Beach.

The walled garden and its three buildings, the sycamore allée, and the pool area collectively comprise the western half of the property. To the east, a long axial greensward begins with a kids' seesaw just beyond the pool house and, widening as it moves northward, arrives at a great lawn and stone terrace overlooked by the rear of the main house. Miranda's mix of landscape elements— the flanking trees, masses of enormous, clipped boxwood,

ABOVE AND OPPOSITE: The gentleman's bath, by contrast, is more restrained and compact. The glazed tile in the shower pairs effectively with the Japanese printed paper interior designer Virginia Tupker found for the walls (*left*). The spare understructure of the washstand reveals an animated marble panel that also serves as a backsplash (*right*).

ABOVE: One of the children's baths, with its curtained tub niche and irresistible pink porcelain washstand. OPPOSITE: In the attic, with its reclaimed timbers and upholstered ceiling and walls, is a cozy playroom for the kids.

appealingly shaggy flowerbeds, and stretches of uncut meadow alternating with manicured grass—is, to my mind, the perfect prelude to the architecture. Like the New England precedents that inspired it, the house remains at once stately and understated: Aware that the decoration would be an eye-popping contrast to the house's structural bones, I took pains to give the exterior the character of lightly worn elegance, the architectural equivalent of those who don't need to think too much about what they're putting on because their sense of style is so innate and flawless. This quality of easy tradition makes the decorative reversal of expectation, once you go inside, all the more satisfying.

Within, the architecture remains determinedly classical, not only in terms of layout, language, and detail, but hierarchically as well, while the decoration, deftly orchestrated by Virginia Tupker, is a slyly brilliant counterpoint of bohemian modernism. The moldings in the entry and adjoining stair hall and library, the restrained elegance of the balusters and bracketed stringers on the stair, all speak of tradition. The 40-foot-long living room with double fireplaces is slightly low-ceilinged (and shallow-beamed) to suggest a single space that might once have been two parlors divided by a center hall (as was often the case in Colonial residences). The more casual glazed sunroom on one end of the main floor's formal core features painted plank walls and a limestone and antique terra-cotta tile floor; and the kitchen/mudroom wing, on the opposite end, is also appropriately less fancy, with beadboard walls and rough-hewn timbers on the ceilings. All of this traditional detail interacts, in surprising sympathy, with patterns, colors, furnishings, and art-

works representing periods both historic and contemporary.

As the guests have their own cottage, the entirety of the second floor is reserved for the family's private quarters; the children's rooms and baths are at one end, while the parents' suite consumes all the remaining square footage, a substantial portion of which is devoted to the wife's charming bath and dressing room. Conceived in the way that Nancy Lancaster would have shaped a similar space in an English manor house, the room is a tour-de-force boudoir, with a floating tub, fireplace lined with Delft tiles, and a grand pedestal sink set between two windows. As for the third floor, with its elegantly proportioned dormers and inward-slanting walls, I envisioned it as an old beamed attic, warm and still, and installed reclaimed timbers to enhance the historic character. It, too, has a little of that manor house feel, as if it were the domain of an English nanny, to which the kids might retreat for tea, biscuits, and scary stories.

But my clients, fun-loving, indefatigable, and endlessly imaginative hosts that they are, had a few additional ideas in mind. After all, there was an entire basement that was rife with possibility. Clearly this was not going to be the usual cobwebby space with old sports equipment and a washing machine; our assignment instead was to create a subterranean spa, as well as a chic spot to go after dinner

ABOVE AND OPPOSITE: A dramatic staircase descends from the house's well-behaved first floor to a swank, glam underworld. Highly reflective black lacquer covers the walls and ceiling; the stair lighting is concealed in the plaster handrail, heightening the sense of mystery as you venture down.

RIGHT: Two back-to-back banquettes, on two different levels, both covered in suede, one serpentine, the other angular. The collections displayed in the bar were dramatically lit by L'Observatoire International, as was the entirety of the room. Designing a party space such as this was not only fun, but an energizing departure from my office's usual work and proved to be an exciting, provocative challenge.

OPPOSITE AND ABOVE: Whether you want to get in shape for an evening in the nightclub or you need to recover from one, an adjacent spa, inspired by a bath in a Lutyens country house, provides yet another subterranean surprise. The spa includes a plunge pool, steam room, sauna, and shower.

PREVIOUS PAGES: The new entertaining barn, positioned at the junction between the main house and guest cottage, replaced a preexisting garage building. When the glass doors are open, the barn becomes a gateway between the two sides of the property. ABOVE AND OPPOSITE: On the house's south side, overlooking the back lawn, sits one of the estate's many outdoor experiences: a long bluestone terrace off the living room. For a family that loves to entertain, one of our objectives was to maximize opportunities to do so in different ways.

for drinks and dancing. When I seemed puzzled about finding the right stylistic avenue to venture down, the wife made it simple: "Just make it louche," she said mischievously, and all became clear. Working side by side with Virginia, we imagined a space reminiscent of London when it was swinging or Paris in the 1980s. There is a bar, a deejay station, a dance floor, a screen for movies, and several lounging areas, all finished in a high-gloss black lacquer with creamy undulating suede banquettes and sexy lighting. And there is also, behind a set of sliding gridded mahogany doors, a handsome teak-and-tile Lutyens-inspired spa, complete with steam room, sauna, showers, and a plunge pool. Design-wise, this subterranean world turned out to be just the sort of challenge I have grown to relish—because it once again pulled me out of my comfort zone and forced me to take my classical principles in new directions.

To undertake a project of this scale and complexity, to work with the most adventurous of clients and able of collaborators—to execute our collective vision at the highest level of quality and detail and without compromise—is an enormous privilege. And the knowledge that the house and its surroundings represent an ever-changing canvas reflective of the residents' zeal for experience and restless creativity makes it that much sweeter. If a house is to be forever, it has to be able to evolve with its owners' lives, tastes, and passions. Life, at its best, remains a work in progress. And if architecture is to reflect the life within it, so it should be as well.

PREVIOUS PAGES: Landscape designer Miranda Brooks crafted the inviting pergola that adjoins the entertaining barn, with the new garage and guesthouse in the near distance (*left*). Details of her appealingly eccentric (and romantic) garden pathways, and one of the conical-roofed pavilions (its mate concealing a pizza oven) that we designed for the garden (*right*). OPPOSITE: A view down an allée of sycamores to the oval-shaped pool and the Palm Beach-meets-Charlottenburg pool pavilion.

LIFE ON THE LOGGIA

Over time, I have found that there is a difference in the way that people approach indoor/outdoor living, especially in warm climates. At the risk of generalizing, most Southerners are tolerant of the heat, even embracing the sultry weather when it comes. On the other hand, my clients from the North, while appreciating the warmth of a tropical location, really love their air-conditioning. So it wasn't surprising that an empty-nester couple from Arkansas, who approached me about a project on the Florida coast, were keenly focused on the exterior living aspects of their proposed residence, regardless of the season—they wanted to be outdoors (even while indoors) as much as possible. At our first meeting, the wife told me that, irrespective of what else we did, the house would pivot around a sizeable central porch where most of their living would occur—a place to sit, to eat, to play games, to be together, or even just to read and be solitary. Indeed, that porch would drive everything else about the architecture.

Their property was somewhat unusual. Though it is, in effect, a suburban lot, it is three acres in size, with a football field's length of beach along South

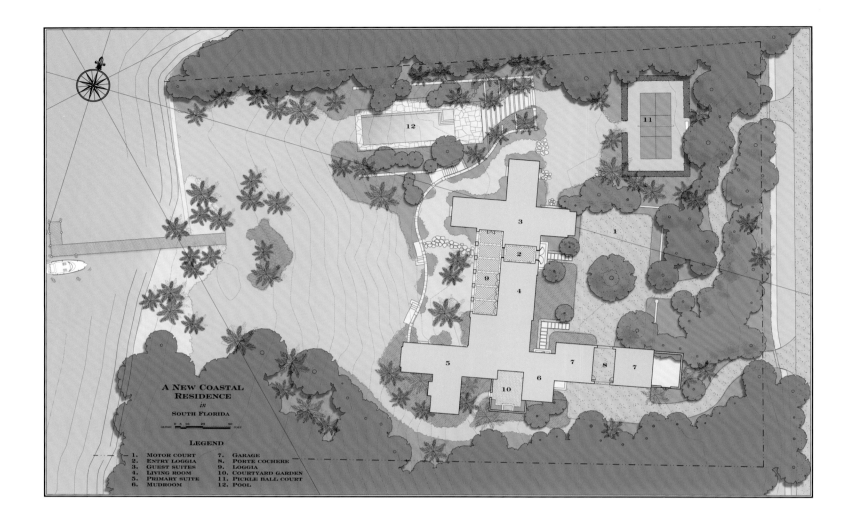

A NEW COASTAL
RESIDENCE
in
SOUTH FLORIDA

LEGEND

1.	MOTOR COURT	7.	GARAGE
2.	ENTRY LOGGIA	8.	PORTE COCHERE
3.	GUEST SUITES	9.	LOGGIA
4.	LIVING ROOM	10.	COURTYARD GARDEN
5.	PRIMARY SUITE	11.	PICKLE BALL COURT
6.	MUDROOM	12.	POOL

Florida's slow-rolling, Intracoastal Waterway. The neighborhood effuses a certain degree of residential formality, a subtly assertive sense of elegant decorum. But I knew that for this couple I'd need to avoid anything overtly classical that might undercut the low-key, laid-back spirit they wanted their home to express.

That spirit stemmed from the memories of a generational compound their family had maintained on the coast of Mississippi, a beloved getaway for holidays and summers where they could enjoy the ostentatious heat, live an outdoor life devoid of extraneous distractions, and steep happily in the sultry atmosphere of the Gulf of Mexico. Sadly, all of that was completely wiped away by Hurricane Katrina, and my clients chose, rather than rebuilding, to relocate, finding the tropical character of Florida to be sympathetic to their way of life. What they didn't want was anything that was formal

or pretentious, but rather a reincarnation of the lazy joys of hot-weather waterside living they'd enjoyed previously.

Though they missed their old place, my clients were too smart (and too sensitive) to show me photographs and say, "Do this." Rather, they trusted me to come up with a new translation of their old family homestead, one that took into account the regional and circumstantial differences without

PAGE 219: The "front door" is a breezeway that gives access to both the main and guest wings (to the left and right, respectively) and serves as a portal to the grounds and, beyond them, the Intracoastal Waterway. PREVIOUS PAGES: An outsize ficus tree commands the entry court. (Beyond it lies the residence's carriage house wing, with its porte cochère.) The shaggy, overgrown landscape supports the idea of a rambling Caribbean house nestled into a tropical setting. ABOVE: The T-shaped structure separates the foreshortened entry court from the expansive, down-sloping back lawn. OPPOSITE: The view from the beach up to the house's water-facing side reveals its commanding six-bay loggia.

sacrificing the spirit of what they had before. Casting about for a suitable template, and knowing that I would always have to keep the formality in check, I looked to the West Indies, Jamaica in particular. I was drawn to the vernacular stucco cottages that, in fact, claim kinship with historic homes in the American South: a series of pavilions mashed up together, with localized symmetry and formality but a general air of seductive disorder, an architectural language that easily accommodates loggias, arcades, and porches. The house we designed in the end is long and rambling, and provides the low-key, informal experience sought by the couple. When you come down the curving drive overhung with shaggy vegetation and arrive in a courtyard framed by the pri-

mary structure and adjoining carriage house (the two together forming an L in plan), what you behold resembles an agglomeration of elegant cottages.

Rather than installing a conventional front door, I chose instead to create a generous open-air entry porch—a kind of breezeway—that is set to the side of the central block of the house, rather than at its center, and separates the main house from the guest wing, offering individual access to each. Several

ABOVE: One of the three pavilion-like guest suites, looking west through two sets of open doors toward the water view. OPPOSITE: A shallow set of broad grass steps descends between palms to the pool, tucked into the landscape at the property's north end.

considerations motivated this decision. The first was purely celebratory: instead of being welcomed by a solid wall of house, you look through it to the broad, downsloping rear garden and, beyond it, the waterway—a casual, sensual, utterly inviting experience that establishes the home's tone in a stroke. My second reason was architectural: opening up a space in the façade, substituting a view for structure, enabled me to "down-mass" the house and make it less imposing. My third idea had to do with the reality of living in an intergenerational residence. When the kids and the grandkids—or even friends—are visiting, the house can be noisy and boisterous, filled with life. But when it's just my clients on the premises, an outsize structure like this one, with all those empty rooms, can feel a bit lonely, and even forbidding. Putting some space between the main house and the guest wing makes the place more manageable and cozy when my clients are home alone— and when they're not, friends and family are just across the breezeway, or upstairs in the carriage house.

I elaborated on the idea of making the house feel smaller in another way. Entering the interior, one finds a long, soaring, and grandly scaled living room—the peaked ceiling supported by four monumental cypress trusses, an homage to ones I had seen by F. Burrall Hoffman, the architect of Vizcaya—and beyond it the bar/pantry, kitchen, and family room. Then the plan makes a turn toward the water, into a wing comprised largely of a study and the primary suite, which projects out toward the Intracoastal and enjoys windows on three sides. Thus, should my clients choose to do so, they can live entirely in their own end of the house, with excursions into the kitchen or outside to the loggia and terrace. And when the house fills up again, they have a place to steal some quiet moments in the day, tucked away from the hubbub. I think it's essential,

PREVIOUS PAGES: To give height and scale to a largely one-story house, we added a partial second floor to the building's primary block, which anchors the overall composition. On the courtyard side, the upstairs is given to attic space; in the back, dormers bring down light into the long loggia. RIGHT: The entry breezeway serves as a stylish arrival moment, set between the tropical heat and the cool interiors of the main and guest wings.

OPPOSITE AND ABOVE: Two views of the living room, looking toward the entry and the attenuated vestibule that connects the space to the front door. Pecky and plain cypress boards panel the walls and ceiling; the muscular ceiling trusses were sampled from the work of F. Burrall Hoffman, architect of Vizcaya.

whenever possible, to build flexibility into a plan—creating ways to be separate and private can be just as important as creating convivial spots for being together.

Let me add that the family/guest wing, on the other side of the breezeway, offers its own considerable charms. Principally these are the pleasures of spatial abundance and a layout made of three individually projecting wings that provide the opportunity for multiple exposures for each room. The three bedrooms have what I would I characterize as Southern proportions. Really tall ceilings. A sense of light and airiness. Pocketing screen doors. And there's even a detail I borrowed from my grandmother's house in south Georgia, where I spent so many happy days as a child: all of the guest suites have louvered outer doors at their entries, to ensure air flow while providing visual privacy—a nod to the days before air-conditioning. At the end of the day, I wanted the house to feel Southern, not just tropical, and to have qualities that serve as an ever-present reminder of my client's roots.

For all of my architectural exertions, my pondering of plan and section and detail, of historic precedents and the future and the past, the real heart of the house isn't within the walls at all. Rather, it is the monumental six-bay loggia that consumes the back of the house overlooking the water, sixty feet in length, sixteen feet deep, fourteen feet at its highest, and always ready for the elements with concealed screens and hurricane shutters. Back in Mississippi, the porch was the thing, and that's what my clients wanted here. And so, you might say, we created a house that is a life-support system for the porch. Indeed, when the screens are put into service, you can fling open the three French doors connecting the living room to the loggia and create a single, super-size indoor/outdoor space. The unfolding experience—from

The living room's opposite side reveals the transom-topped portals to the butler's pantry and bar, at left, and the kitchen on the right—rooms that feel accessible but not intrusive. Light streams in from glazing on both sides; the windows to the right can be opened completely to the adjoining loggia to create an incomparable indoor/outdoor experience.

RIGHT: A view of the kitchen, with its colossal enameled metal range hood. The double-sided glass cabinetry above one of the room's two sinks lightly separates the space from the adjoining breakfast room. FOLLOWING PAGES: The kitchen's pass-through frames a view of the garden (*left*). Just beyond, the breakfast room has a casual painted floor, one of several that decorative painter Bob Christian created for the interior (*right*). The house's relaxed character precluded a formal dining room: the residents eat here, or out on the loggia.

234

OPPOSITE: The relaxed, comfortable mood of the family room, immediately adjacent to the kitchen, flows naturally out to the dining area on the loggia. Large glazed doors pocket completely into the walls, uniting the spaces. ABOVE: Prior to design development, the family expressed an interest in making the loggia the house's focal point. They got their wish. (Motorized screens within the arches descend to render the space bug-free in the evenings.)

OPPOSITE AND ABOVE: At the loggia's north end, beyond the hanging swing sofas—which recall similar ones at the family's previous home in Mississippi— French doors connect to the guest wing. Light filters down from dormers in the big central hipped roof above that open into the loggia ceiling.

OPPOSITE AND ABOVE: The primary suite is separated from an adjoining gallery by an expansive elliptical archway. A lofty tray ceiling and windows on three sides invest the space with a character at once airy and romantic. The French doors open onto a lawn terrace overlooking the water.

LEFT: A view of a guest suite from the garden. OPPOSITE: The hallway in the guest wing. Louvered doors at the entrance to each suite facilitate cooling air flow while ensuring privacy. Bob Christian painted the playful decorative floor runner.

living room to loggia to lawn to waterway—is truly special, and something I'd not been able to do before. I think of it as a celebration of life at its sweetest.

I collaborated with two wonderful partners for this project: Jane Schwab for the interiors and Cecilia de Grelle for the landscape. Jane, an accomplished designer and a long-time friend of the couple, knew their history well and understood their decorative sensibility perfectly. Forsaking the expected tropical hues, Jane and the wife chose a highly distilled palette of serene whites and creams, punctuated by equally gentle doses of soft greens, blues, and yellows. The interiors are bright and airy, designed to collect—and reflect—the sun and infuse the relaxed atmosphere with warmth and light. And as we endeavored to do with the architecture, the interiors present an unfussiness that never competes with the energy of the landscape just outside.

I'd worked with Cecilia before, on projects in both Florida and Maine, and was delighted to be partnered with her again; here, her brief was similar to mine, in that anything that smacked of too much formality would be unacceptable. Cecilia's general preference is for an unmanicured, relaxed landscape—in this regard, she was in perfect sync with our clients—and that is what you see as you enter the property, where she removed much of the preexisting clipped hedges and manicured vegetation emblematic of the region, favoring instead a plant selection that is tropical and jungle-like along the new S-shaped entry drive. The rear terrace, the lawn that descends down to the water, and the various spaces around each of the bedroom wings, conversely, present a more composed yet offhand elegance. And the pool, reached by a broad, shallow slope of coquina stone stairs set in the lawn and tucked behind a rise in the land, presided over by stands of tall old palms, offers a tableau worthy of Slim Aarons at his midcentury finest. Indeed, the landscape remains as varied as the architecture, and, I think, partners with it perfectly.

Like the celebrated English architect Edwin Lutyens, I have always believed that great clients make great houses, and that is perhaps especially the case in this instance. I found myself so inspired by this couple's character—their history and their desire to move it forward, their imagination and willingness to try new things in the service of a tireless joy in life—and I believe the outcome is as much due to their sensibility as it is to my efforts. That, I think, represents the practice of architecture at its most effective—something for which my office strives every time we meet new clients, visit their sites, and listen to their dreams.

ABOVE: A guest wing passageway reveals walk-in closets styled as wardrobe cabinets with louvered doors. RIGHT: Like the primary suite, the guest bedrooms enjoy high ceilings, light on three sides, and easy access to the garden—all hallmarks of classic Southern living. FOLLOWING PAGES: The seductive elegance of the pool is enhanced by an air of privacy: the pool is set apart from the rest of the property, secluded by towering palms and lush plantings.

SHIP SHAPE

What happens when an old building must find a new purpose in life? I'm sure many of you, like myself, have come across structures like this at one point or another: an old church that's become a residence, or a firehouse reincarnated as a restaurant. I've always been intrigued by this particular architectural assignment, because of my curiosity about the design process, which I think is even trickier when a nonresidential building is converted into a home. What will the big architectural idea be? What has to be eliminated, what is to be kept? How do you find the balance between preserving the aesthetic and historic character of the original while creating a satisfying new experience, one that feels authentically like a dwelling? And perhaps most intriguingly: How does the architect shape a private residential space that still somehow acknowledges its presence in the public realm?

I finally got my chance to dig into these issues with a project of precisely this character, in a seemingly unassuming building that turned out to be extraordinary. The answers I discovered were not always obvious or easily arrived at, but their pursuit ignited my creativity in totally unexpected and quite wonderful ways.

First, a bit of backstory, as I came to know it: At the end of the nineteenth century, a young man named Chauncey Borland, while in the midst of his studies at Harvard, decided to commission a steam yacht for jaunts between Boston and the coast of Maine, where his family had a summer cottage. The scion of a wealthy

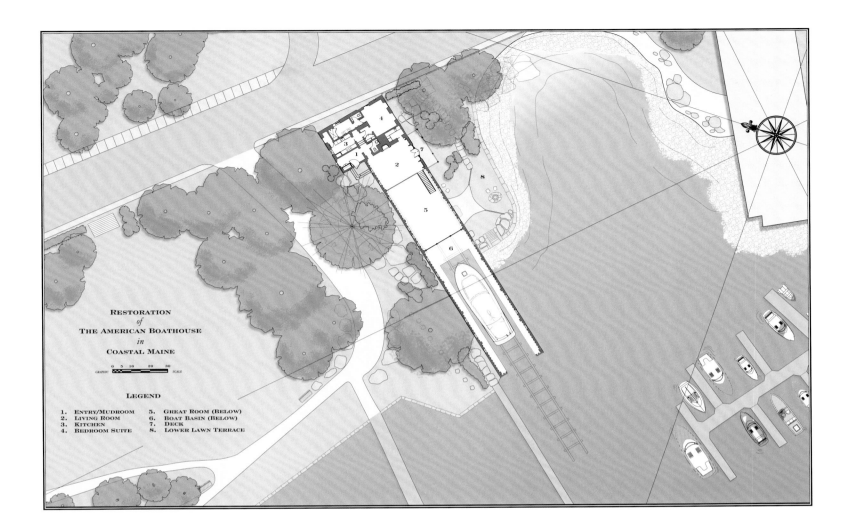

RESTORATION
of
THE AMERICAN BOATHOUSE
in
COASTAL MAINE

0 5 10   20   30
GRAPHIC   SCALE

LEGEND

1. ENTRY/MUDROOM   5. GREAT ROOM (BELOW)
2. LIVING ROOM   6. BOAT BASIN (BELOW)
3. KITCHEN   7. DECK
4. BEDROOM SUITE   8. LOWER LAWN TERRACE

Chicago clan, Borland engaged Arthur Binney, an MIT-trained, Boston-based naval architect, who duly produced a craft, the *Imago*, for him in 1899. Following Borland's graduation in 1901, he again called upon Binney's services, this time to design a larger, more elegant boat that he christened the *Monaloa*. As the indefatigable young Borland progressed through his twenties, he kept upgrading his fleet, following his second craft with an even bigger commission, in 1904, for the *Monaloa II*.

Faced with needing to shelter a boat of substantial size (the *Monaloa II* was roughly one hundred feet in length) in the off-season, Borland decided to commission the construction of a

PAGE 250: The water-facing side of the boathouse, seen through a romantic tableau of masts and fog. OPPOSITE AND ABOVE: The building occupies a unique position on this Down East harbor, at once public and private, with direct access to the water for the owners' boat.

boathouse, to be built on his town's harbor—one big enough to enclose the craft in its entirety during the harsh Maine winter months. The boathouse, positioned among a number of similarly sized and purposed structures, all built in the early years of the twentieth century on the northern end of the harbor, was quite long: it sloped all the way down from the street to the water's edge, a 150-foot transit. It was also large enough to enclose the full height and length of the last two *Monaloa*s (the third, in 1909, came in at 105 feet long), and of sufficient length to reach into the harbor, so that the yachts could float directly into the building.

Getting a boat of this size into its shelter was no small feat, and required quite a bit of innovation. A railroad track, atop which sat a huge cradle, extended from the building down into the harbor; when it came time to berth the craft, Borland's crew would maneuver the bow into the cradle, which would then be hauled by great chains into the boathouse's long interior. Those chains were attached to a winch system that, in turn, was connected via a shaft to a capstan and gears in the building's headhouse (the work rooms and offices facing the street). Once the boat was cradled, a team of mules or oxen, yoked to the capstan, would do the pulling by walking in a circle and turning the gears. It sounds primitive to our twenty-first-century ears, but in 1904 it was the height of modernity.

The *Monaloa III* was requisitioned by the US Navy in 1917 for deployment in World War I, but was back in private use by the 1920s—and from there we jump forward in time to 1973. By then the boathouse, long abandoned, had fallen into disrepair, when it found a champion in Kenneth Carlson, a retired advertising executive who fell in love with the building and purchased it to prevent its demolition. Discovering that it was one of Maine's oldest extant marine shelters, Carlson had it listed on the National Register of Historic Places. And he gave it a name: the American Boathouse.

By the time I first saw the structure, over forty years later and more than a century after its construction, the once-formidable shelter had shed all of its mercantile glamour. Though a landmark, the boathouse had become a picturesque ruin: used from time to time by one or another boatbuilder or carpenter (who added random additions to the exterior and inserted equally random provisional structures into the interior), a repository for junk of every sort, inhabited by armies of birds and other creatures, and on the verge of collapse.

Who could resist? Not my clients, it turns out. Boat owners themselves, passionate about the local architectural history, and people of considerable vision, they saw the derelict structure—

which had been put up for sale—as an opportunity to do something very singular and special, while preserving a piece of the town's historic fabric. Their own boat was considerably smaller than the last iteration of the *Monaloa*, which meant that the interior could be used as a boathouse, but also thought about in new ways. Happily, my clients asked me to consider how the building might be converted into a more domestic environment, while also sheltering their craft in the off-season. The idea was to use roughly half the space as a boat basin, and the rest as a guesthouse, a place for entertaining, and, in my imagination at least, a Captain Nemo-esque lair. I was initially overwhelmed by the scale of the building's interior and the amount of work required to keep the place from falling down. But then I remembered all those great examples of adaptive reuse I'd seen over the years on the streets of New York and elsewhere and became tremendously excited by—indeed, grateful for—this challenging opportunity. And so my team and I dove in.

Before we hit the creative water, however, a number of requirements related to local zoning and the building's protected status had to be satisfied. Surprisingly, permission to use part of the space as a residence demanded that a zoning amendment be put to a public vote. (Thankfully, it passed.) And because the boathouse was landmarked, there could be no changes whatsoever to the original design of the exterior. It was my good fortune that our landscape architect on two other recent Maine projects, the endlessly resourceful Stephen Mohr, had worked extensively on restoration projects and knew the ins and outs of navigating the complex process of restoring and altering a landmarked building in Maine. Working hand-in-glove with our builder, the equally talented and capable Jay Fischer, we were able to take the

OPPOSITE: Historic photos of the *Monaloa III*, one of the boathouse's original residents, in the harbor in the 1920s (*top*) and as it was being reunited with its home berth following its decommissioning after World War I (*bottom*). ABOVE: The structure, originally designed to accommodate yachts that filled it entirely, has a monumental scale that enabled us to divide the interior, giving half to a boat slip and the rest to the residence (visible through the soaring glass wall beyond the boat cradle).

ABOVE: A small library, with its English reading table, is tucked under the mezzanine. The flanking walls of the space are lined with reproductions of the original drawings of the *Monaloa I, II,* and *III,* discovered in the archives at MIT. RIGHT: The boathouse is entered at the mezzanine level, and you pass through a sitting/dining area to descend to the grandly scaled, cathedral-like primary entertaining space, with its 23-foot-high ceiling. The windows, set high, create a sense of mystery from the outside regarding what actually lies within.

ABOVE: A vitrine on the lower level showcases the original winch mechanism used to haul in the various iterations of the *Monaloa*. OPPOSITE: Dramatic illumination by lighting designer Nathan Orsman makes the boat feel like a giant sea creature lurking just beyond the precinct of the interior—a motor yacht by day, an objet d'art after hours.

OPPOSITE AND ABOVE: Two views of the mezzanine, with its inviting fireplace at the center of the cozy sitting area. Easy access to a snug bar makes this space especially appealing. We found the pair of 1940s Italian mahogany-and-suede steamer chairs in New York and had the geometrically graphic rug made for the room.

RIGHT AND OPPOSITE: As much attention was paid to the detailing and decoration of the boathouse as was given to the architecture, the better to convey the sense that it is the lair of well-traveled individuals, each with a good eye and a taste for the unusual and unexpected. In particular, we sought out the arrestingly quirky and the specifically maritime, including portholes in the lower-level doors, a large eighteenth-century anchor, and reclaimed wood beams and planking throughout.

structure apart, salvage as many of the original architectural, material, and structural elements as possible, and put it all back together again while adhering to contemporary building codes. Getting the state's blessing and following the rules of historic preservation were challenges of no small consequence. But Stephen and Jay, in the end, achieved a remarkable outcome: a thoroughly new envelope that looks precisely as it did at the dawn of the twentieth century.

Within, aware that the introduction of essential structural materials like concrete and steel might give the space an industrial feel that could be misread as high-tech, I sought to preserve those original architectural elements that blended drama and history. On my initial visit, I was immediately drawn to the rhythmically deployed angled wood braces in the upper part of the interior that originally supported the roof: they gave the vast space, with its twenty-three-foot-high ceiling, the flavor of a cathedral, and though their function would be superseded by the concealed steel framing, I wanted to keep them in place.

As noted, the building slopes downward as it moves from land toward the water, with the original headhouse zone at the highest elevation, fronting onto the public street. Given the great ceiling height of the boathouse's main volume, we were able to construct a mezzanine that extends outward from the headhouse and combines with it to form a capacious upper level. The headhouse has been transformed into the building's primary residential zone: off the entry, one finds a powder room, and beyond that, the kitchen and bedroom suite. As for the adjoining mezzanine (which overlooks the lower level and the boat basin), it serves as the living/dining room, with a snug and welcoming bar tucked behind the fireplace.

If the mezzanine offers one sort of drama, the main floor below (accessed by a wood-and-steel stair) delivers an excitement all its own. What might be characterized as the back-of-house area, situated beneath the old headhouse, is largely devoted to function (catering kitchen, bathrooms, laundry, storage)—with a twist: the old winch mechanism has been reinstalled in roughly its original location, now in a glass-enclosed room like a vitrine, to create an arresting surprise that gives visitors a glimpse of the boathouse's unique history. I also lined this space with framed prints of the original naval architectural drawings for all three of the *Monaloas*, found in the archives at MIT.

The rest of the lower level is devoted to the appropriately named great room. A cozy area beneath the mezzanine serves as a library/study, while the full-height zone functions as a sitting room, made all the more spectacular by the building's most virtuoso element: a twenty-five-foot-high glass wall, behind which my clients' own Hinckley picnic boat rests, when it's not on the water, like a sleek animal, in the ecclesiastical space of the basin. To sit in the great room is a truly sublime experience: charged silence interrupted only by the occasional marine motor or foghorn; furnishings and collected objects as diverse as they are fascinating; and, a transparent membrane beyond which lies the boat and, still beyond that, the harbor. It is a moment out of Jules Verne (or, perhaps, James Bond).

Though it might sound funny for an architect to admit this, the supreme pleasure of this project lay not simply in devising the space but also in filling it up. My clients are unique individuals: exceptionally well-read and cerebral, committed world travelers, and discerning connoisseurs of art, craft, and culture. Thus, instead of setting out to decorate the boathouse, they saw it more as a cabinet of curiosities to be filled with the relics of life's journeys. We took our time, using their travels to find the quirky and the beautiful, the delightful and the bizarre, creating a calm but fantastical, fascinating inner world.

Many of the original windows of the long structure that stretches down to the water are set well above most of the living spaces, contributing to the sense of the boathouse as a rarefied, almost secret environment. Yet the place continues to have a strong presence in the town: its western face anchors the edge of a town park, the exterior in clear view of the street and the public lawn that abuts it. This relic of the harbor's formative years, though private property, remains a still significant piece in the mosaic of a town's—and a region's—colorful history, now preserved to last another century or more.

OPPOSITE: The modest, and modestly-scaled, entry foyer gives no hint of what lies beyond.

264

ABOVE: We commissioned ceramicist Joan Platt to make all the dishware for the boathouse, her last project before shuttering her pottery studio. OPPOSITE: The window at the kitchen's far end reads as a glazed door on the outside; because the building is landmarked, we were prohibited from making any changes to the exterior, doors and windows included. Hand-troweled plaster and rustic reclaimed beams preserve the structure's mercantile character. The floor replicates the pine planks found in the original. The abstract elegance of the artwork and carefully arranged tableaux give the room an air of serenity and sophistication.

ABOVE AND OPPOSITE: For all of its spatial extravagance, the boathouse contains a single bedroom, with an ensuite companion bath. The surprising appearance of a Japanese screen, discovered by the owners in Europe, contributes to the presiding global flavor of the interiors. The bath's metal dish lantern expresses the nautical character of the building's history—and its architecture.

THE LONG VIEW

One of the poignant things about a multigenerational residence is that it is born out of dreams that have often taken root long before the generations that will fill its rooms have begun to gestate. Indeed, in this instance, the dream of a family home began as an idea, one passed along from a father to his son.

This house sits upon a truly unique property, a bluff that rises some twenty feet above Lake Champlain, embracing showstopping views across the water to the Adirondack Mountains and northward to the wilds of Canada. My client, who was born and raised in this New England region, was encouraged to purchase the land (which included an undistinguished ranch house, very close to the water) by his father. The elder man was a banker of the old school, conservative and prudent, who nudged his son to buy the land even though he and his wife were decades away from having the wherewithal to develop it. "It's a great piece of property," observed the father when the acreage came up for auction. "Someday you'll do something with it." Fortuitously, my client heeded this parental advice.

Time passed, and those future generations began to appear—children, grandchildren, nieces, and nephews by the multitude, many living alongside their land, or else nearby in the region. More time passed, and my clients became the relatives to whom the generations gravitated, on the holidays to be sure, but also occasions less seasonal but no less special. And when, eventually, the time was right

A New Residence
on
Lake Champlain, Vermont

GRAPHIC SCALE 0 25 50 100

LEGEND

1. Entry Court
2. Main House
3. Guesthouse
4. Bunkhouse
5. Lake Barn
6. Beach Haus
7. Tennis House/Potting Shed
8. Vegetable Garden

to "do something," they decided to build not merely a house, but a gathering place: a dwelling where everyone would be welcome, not in a fixed, formal way, but instead in a fun and, especially, flexible mode. A place, moreover, where the phrases "sorry, there's no more room" and "that's precious, don't touch" would never be uttered.

The plan was to demolish the existing ranch house and replace it with a building large enough to accommodate this vision—which presented me, architecturally, with a pair of interesting challenges. The first involved zoning. The husband loved the existing structure's close proximity to the water and wanted to build on its site, the better to maximize the views. The thorny issue was that the new house would be considerably larger than what was there already, and while we could legally occupy the old footprint (and planned to do so), the setback lines (which dictated how close you could build to the water) had changed. This meant that the rest of the structure would have to ramble back-

ward from the undulating shoreline, forming a kind of parabola that seemed to work against a coherent floor plan.

The second challenge was stylistic and grew out of the first. The wife, the daughter of an antiques dealer and herself well-schooled in Early American decorative arts and architecture, had her heart set on a prototypical foursquare Colonial New England house. Unfortunately, this particular style would be next to impossible to replicate, given the contortions imposed by the new

PAGE 270: The complex of buildings sits on a low, picturesque bluff on the shore of Lake Champlain, with commanding views of the Adirondack Mountains and the setting sun. PREVIOUS PAGES: The eccentric plan of the house reflects the zoning mandate, with the primary wing on the footprint of a previous structure, and the others folded back from the bluff. ABOVE: The site plan reveals the interweaving of landscape and buildings. OPPOSITE: The front porch and the entry door, which affords, upon arrival, the first tantalizing glimpse of the lake.

PREVIOUS PAGES: The house's details reveal a combination of the local vernacular architecture and more tightly tailored Federal and Colonial Revival precedents. We drew inspiration from a range of regional historic structures, in particular the houses found at the nearby Shelburne Museum, including the 'Vermont House,' with its distinctive stone façade. ABOVE AND OPPOSITE: Two views of the entry hall, one revealing the Dutch front door, with its sidelights, transom, and robust hardware, the other looking through the living room to the bluff and the lake.

ABOVE: The stair's tapered mahogany balusters reflect a Shaker-style simplicity, paired with more exuberant wave-form stringer brackets. OPPOSITE: A deep Federal arch connects the entry to the stair hall and, just beyond, a large butler's pantry.

RIGHT: One end of the paneled living room, with its collection of antiques found in New England and old England as well. In keeping with the family's desire for an informal environment, the house is furnished handsomely but not fancily—emphasizing comfort, utility, and a welcoming spirit.

ABOVE: The large portal between the living and dining rooms answered our clients' wish to have the public spaces feel flowing and interconnected. Light and views are present everywhere in the house. OPPOSITE: Another view of the living room reveals the omnipresence of the water. The serene, neutral palette reflects the predilections of the owners.

RIGHT: The dining room is deliberately scaled for large gatherings, as befits a residence meant to serve as a multigenerational family retreat. The pocket door at the room's far side connects to the kitchen and family room beyond; French doors at left open onto a long lakeside porch, where another dining table is set up for alfresco meals.

ABOVE: The glazed hallway connects the primary and guest wings and terminates in a bedroom suite, framing a welcoming view of the room's fireplace. A small porch lies just outside the glass doors to the right, providing yet another spot from which to enjoy views of the water. OPPOSITE: The pine-paneled library—the hinge between the house's main volume and the guest wing—features a book-lined hidden door that gives access to a secret study.

ABOVE AND OPPOSITE: A grand and well-appointed bedroom on the ground floor of the guest wing features a cozy sitting area with windows on three sides and lake views. Over the room's eighteenth-century Swedish chest, a nineteenth-century "sailor's valentine" found on Nantucket.

OPPOSITE AND ABOVE: The ground-floor guest bedroom's adjoining bath—as graciously scaled as the room itself—includes a soaking tub flanked by double sinks, all beneath a high cove ceiling. The room captures the quality of comfortable abundance found throughout the house.

ABOVE AND OPPOSITE: Everything in the kitchen is designed to support large, convivial gatherings of family and friends. A built-in sideboard with a butcher-block top and ample cabinet and drawer space lightly separates the space (with its grand island) from the family room.

RIGHT: A bay window in the kitchen overlooking the water is home to a cozy banquette and breakfast table. One might prefer the cushioned seat beneath the windows for reasons of comfort, but it's the chairs that get the view.

PREVIOUS PAGES: At one end of the family
room, an octagonal bay embraces sweeping,
panoramic vistas of the bluff and Lake
Champlain. RIGHT: The family room's
opposite end, off the kitchen, is dominated
by a muscular fireplace (and its adjoining
stone-lined, log-storage niche). It's a big
room for a big family, consuming the entire
north end of the residence's primary wing.

ABOVE: An indoor "potting shed" and flower room enriched by plenty of open shelving and a deep work sink, custom-made from slabs of black granite. OPPOSITE: The mudroom is effectively a glazed link between the garage wing and the main house. The space offers multiple points of entry, affording egress from different sides of the house and grounds.

RIGHT: The second-floor primary suite bedroom enjoys a private octagonal porch. The French doors, transom, and sidelights effectively convert the entire wall to glass, enhancing the indoor/outdoor connection.

OPPOSITE AND ABOVE: One of the second-floor guest bedrooms gets its comfort and charm from the reader-friendly window seat and pretty printed English wall fabric.

RIGHT: A guest room tucked into another of the house's octagonal wings. Unusually, the profile of the tray ceiling is drawn in lime-washed, rough-hewn beams, which makes an interesting contrast with the elegant furnishings and decorative toile fabric on the walls.

ABOVE AND OPPOSITE: Tucked into the second floor above the garages, the bunkhouse has its own constituency—the youngest generation—and, accordingly, its own personality. A corridor leading from the main house connects to a lofty sitting room, lit by a cupola, and distinguished by visually striking exposed roof framing. The space is open to both a sleeping porch and the bunkroom, and together they sleep twelve.

RIGHT: Evoking the feeling of a summer camp, the eight-bed bunkroom, outfitted with identical iron bedframes, trunks, and night tables, is a great favorite of the extended family's children.

ABOVE: One of the two bunk house baths, this one for the girls. OPPOSITE: The considerable pleasures of the bunkroom derive in large measure from its decoration, which includes numbered towels for each bed—and its occupant.

ABOVE: The second-floor octagonal primary bedroom porch perches atop the screen porch. OPPOSITE: The table we designed for the waterside dining porch divides in two, and offers a maximum capacity of twenty-four. A screen porch lies just beyond.

setback lines, not to mention the needs of the substantial program. As an alternative, I proposed a design in the Shingle Style, a rambling, idiosyncratic typology better suited to a footprint that, because of the zoning rules, had itself to be rambling and idiosyncratic. This, of course, remained precisely at odds with her dream, a circumstance further complicated by the husband's wish to see the water from every room, and their joint desire to be able to make parts of the place private when necessary, yet also to have everything seamlessly, organically integrated.

For inspiration—and a way out of this stylistic quagmire—my clients and I visited Vermont's Shelburne Museum, a remarkable repository of the state's eighteenth- and nineteenth-century residential architecture. The wife had expressed an interest in constructing a part of the house from stone, and when the museum's collection of buildings yielded a winning example of what she had in mind—with the stone laid in a distinctive mosaic pattern—we had a place to begin. From the drawing board, there emerged an exciting hybrid: a tripartite structure concealing what is actually a rambling massing evocative of the Shingle Style, but rendered in a Colonial Revival vocabulary articulated with Federal details and proportions. The main, center volume is distinguished by three side-by-side cross gables that rise up above a long covered front porch; to its right, a five-bay garage building features elliptical arched barn doors inspired by ones we had seen at the Shelburne Museum, giving it the character of an old carriage house. The garage is topped by what we called the "bunkhouse," an informal space that sleeps twelve, and the entirety is connected to the main house by a slender link that serves as the house's mudroom entrance, with a back stair. Sited the left of the center volume, the stone-clad guesthouse features a tower topped by a glazed aerie affording views in all directions.

In the end, we did use shingles to clad the house, and they accomplish what they're traditionally meant to do—that is, to serve as a unifying wrapper—but we painted them a subtly warm white reminiscent of those clapboarded white farmhouses you see throughout Vermont. Overall, the effect is of a house born in the late Colonial era that evolved, in picturesque fashion, over time.

The floor plan appropriately reflects a home designed from the inside out, as my clients were much more interested in the placement of the rooms and how they related to one another and the water—the experience—than the appearance of the exterior elevations. This is immediately apparent upon entering, as the view from the front door looks straight through the house to the lake beyond, creating a stunning moment of welcome. Past the entry hall, the graciously scaled public spaces unfold in an enfilade, with the living and dining rooms, a big communal kitchen, and family room all opening onto one another; the upstairs is loosely zoned into a primary suite and three additional guest bedrooms. Back on the ground floor, a long lake-facing porch, connecting a pair of projecting octagonal wings, unites the two sides of the house and offers panoramic water, mountain, and wilderness vistas.

Unless it's been closed off for the use of a family—simply by shutting a door—the guest cottage is, in fact, fully integrated into the overall experience, with a library, office, kitchenette, and bedroom suite on the ground floor, and another bedroom and gym up above. (The tower room, which rises above the entirety, functions as a cozy getaway for reading, cocktails, or the pleasure of contemplating the view.) On the other side of the house's central section, above the garage, an eight-bed bunkroom enjoys its own living room/kitchen, a sleeping porch that sleeps another four, and boys' and girls' bathrooms. Above and below, from end to end, the wraparound nature of the site and the resulting setbacks enabled us to bring in light and views on every point of the compass; the flow, supported by enfilades from end to end, feels resolved and natural. While the house formally sleeps twenty-four, the number of people is never limited by the number of beds. If the house—and the family—have a motto, it is, without question, "Come one, come all."

With an eye toward extracting the maximum in experience and pleasure from their property, my clients and I developed three additional supporting structures. The most significant is a big stone lake barn, sited on a point of land looking north, that

OPPOSITE: Landscape designer Deborah Nevins created a meadow that affords a view to—and through—the entertaining barn from the entry drive. The large glass doors frame the water vista.

ABOVE: The entertaining barn's entry vestibule, with reclaimed wood siding and a beamed ceiling. OPPOSITE: The building has many uses. It is at once a hangout space, a getaway, and a venue for big meals and family occasions when the main house dining table is insufficient. Two massive stone fireplaces anchor each end of the lofty space, with ceiling trusses inspired by Scandinavian barns (a tip of the hat to the wife's northern European roots).

ABOVE: Twelve-foot-tall glass doors slide completely into the walls, allowing the room to connect to the lake with stunning immediacy. OPPOSITE: A daybed in the corner, next to one of the fireplaces, offers the perfect spot for an afternoon nap.

OPPOSITE AND ABOVE: The entertaining barn's kitchen is rendered in a simple language of open shelves and cabinetry, Shaker-style furniture, and quotidian floorboards and beams.

RIGHT AND OPPOSITE: Details in the entertaining barn reflect its simplicity, rusticity, and utility, encapsulating the rural-agrarian structures that, once upon a time, were ubiquitous in this bucolic corner of New England.

offers an entirely different set of views from those captured by the house and its western outlook. Centered around a great room with double fireplaces, featuring twelve-foot-high windows that pocket into the walls, the barn's standout feature is a seventeen-foot-long dining table, discovered in Antwerp, for hosting family feasts for twenty-plus revelers (as opposed to the main house table, which seats a mere sixteen). Near the entrance to the property from the public road, we inserted a combination tennis pavilion (for the court)/potting shed (for the vegetable garden), distinguished by an open loggia and two solid ends. (This structure finds use in both summer and winter, as the family, with their characteristic sense of mischief and fun, flood the tennis court during the cold months to create an ice rink.) And on the waterfront, there's a playful

folly dubbed the "beach-haus" (in acknowledgment of the wife's northern European roots)—ideal for barbecues and bonfires, swimming off the dock, and the occasional overnight campout.

In close collaboration with our clients and their longtime decorator, Patti Smith, we also applied ourselves to the interior decoration, together seeking out eighteenth- and nineteenth-century English, American, and Scandinavian antiques on shopping trips on both sides of the Atlantic—finds that would complement the delicacy of the Federal architectural details, but never feel too fancy. While certain pieces might fairly be characterized as elegant, most of the selections are quite simple, deriving their appeal more from craft, silhouette, and materiality than from pedigree. As the wife is a discerning collector of antique textiles, we also had the great pleasure of using some of her collection to recover the upholstered pieces—always in the spirit of having fun, personalizing the experience of the home, and avoiding fussiness and the unwelcome prohibitions of anything "precious."

This story would be most incomplete without acknowledging the always indispensable contributions of my longtime collaborator, landscape designer Deborah Nevins. You might think that, on such sublime acreage, any human intervention would be superfluous; but Debby, as ever, found ways to add variety and mystery to the natural setting. Her work proves most impactful upon arrival: pulling into the long driveway, passing the tennis court and vegetable garden, one finds Debby's surprising open meadow—created by clearing some of the densely wooded land—which now frames a tantalizing glimpse of Lake Champlain through the barn's overscale glass doors. And then it's back into the woods before rounding a small knoll into the house's entry court. As an architect, I always try to withhold the spectacular payoff of a view until the very moment one comes through the front door (a gambit learned from Edwin Lutyens). Debby, in step with this idea, achieves the same excitement via her subtle manipulation of landscape. The effect—with this house in particular, where one landscape moments leads to the next—is utterly magical.

And so what began as a gift, in the form of sound advice from father to son, has become the son's gift to multiple generations that follow him both today and for many years to come. Playing the long game with their dream, my clients matured into an understanding of what truly matters in a dwelling: not the bright, shiny objects of high style, but the deep, savory pleasures of everyday life; not a house that imposes itself upon its occupants, but a thoughtfully made container for the most profound and lasting joys. As the old saying goes, one's day will come. I suppose that's not always true, but in this case it certainly did, and it was my great privilege—and pleasure—to help turn someone's aspiration into satisfaction. Truly, for an architect, there's no greater gift.

ABOVE: During the winter, my enterprising clients flood the tennis court, transforming it into an impromptu ice hockey rink. I'm constantly delighted by this and the many other photos sent to me by the family over the years, sharing with me and my team the pleasure they get from their home. OPPOSITE: An evening view of the Adirondacks from the shoreline.

RESOURCES

ANTIQUE- AND RECLAIMED-WOOD FLOORS

Baba Antique Wooden Floors
baba.com

Exquisite Surfaces
xsurfaces.com

The Hudson Company
thehudsonco.com

LaPolla Inspired Flooring
inspiredflooring.com

Natural Creations
realhardwoodfloors.com

ANTIQUE AND REPRODUCTION MANTELS

A & R Asta *(antique wood and stone)*
astafireplaces.com

Chesneys
(antique and reproduction stone)
chesneys.com

Francis J. Purcell
(antique American wood)
francisjpurcell.com

Jamb *(antique and reproduction stone)*
jamb.co.uk

ANTIQUE DEALERS, AUCTION HOUSES, AND DESIGN SHOP FAVORITES

1stdibs
1stdibs.com

Ann-Morris
ann-morris.com

Antique & Art Exchange
antiqueandartexchange.com

Authentic Provence
authenticprovence.com

AvW Antiques
avwantiques.co.uk

Balsamo
balsamoantiques.com

Bamboo&Rattan
vintagebamboorattan.com

Bardith
bardith.com

BK Antiques
bkantiques.com

Blackman Cruz
blackmancruz.com

Bonhams
bonhams.com

Briggs House Antiques
briggshouse.com

Brunk Auctions
brunkauctions.com

Burden
jonathanburden.com

Casa Gusto
getthegusto.com

Christie's
christies.com

Christopher Butterworth
christopherbutterworth.com

C. J. Peters
cjpeters.net

Copley Fine Art Auctions
copleyart.com

Cove Landing
covelanding@gmail.com

David Bedale Antiques
davidbedale.com

Démiurge New York
demiurgenewyork.com

Doyle
doyle.com

Dreweatts
dreweatts.com

The Elephant's Foot Antiques
theelephantsfootantiques.com

English Accent Antiques
englishaccentantiques.com

Faustina Pace Antiques
faustinapace.com

Foster & Gane
fosterandgane.com

Foxglove Antiques & Galleries
foxgloveantiques.com

Galerie Half
galeriehalf.com

Gerald Bland
geraldblandinc.com

Guinevere Antiques
guinevere.co.uk

Harbinger
harbingerla.com

Hollywood at Home
hollywoodathome.com

Howe
howelondon.com

Humphrey Carrasco
humphreycarrasco.com

InCollect
incollect.com

Jayne Thompson Antiques
jaynethompsonantiques.com

JF Chen
jfchen.com

John Bird Antiques
johnbirdantiques.com

KRB
krbnyc.com

Lee Stanton
leestanton.com

Lucca Antiques
luccaantiques.com

March
marchsf.com

Max Rollitt
maxrollitt.com

Michael Trapp
shopmichaeltrapp.com

Nickey Kehoe
nickeykehoe.com

Object
object-la.com

O'Sullivan Antiques
osullivanantiques.com

Pat McGann
patmcganngallery.com

Plain Goods
plain-goods.com

Privet House
privethouse.com

Puckhaber
puckhaberdecorativeantiques.com

Rago
ragoarts.com

Regan & Smith
reganandsmith.com

Robuck
robuck.co

Rose Uniacke
roseuniacke.com

Sibyl Colefax & John Fowler
sibylcolefax.com

Sotheby's
sothebys.com

Spencer Swaffer Antiques
spencerswaffer.com

Stair
stairgalleries.com

Sutter Antiques
sutterantiques.com

Swann Auction Galleries
swanngalleries.com

William Laman
williamlaman.com

William Word Fine Antiques
williamwordantiques.com

Woodnutt Antiques
woodnuttantiques.com

Wright
wright20.com

Wyeth
wyeth.nyc

Yew Tree House Antiques
yewtreehouseantiques.com

CARPETS
(NEW AND ANTIQUE)

Beauvais
beauvaiscarpets.com

Elizabeth Eakins
elizabetheakins.com

Galerie Shabab
galerieshabab.com

Mitchell Denburg Collection
mitchelldenburg.com

The New England Collection
necrugs.com

Robert Kime
robertkime.com

Sacco
saccocarpet.com

Woodard & Greenstein
woodardweave.com

Woven
wovenonline.com

COLOR CONSULTING
AND PAINTS

Benjamin Moore
benjaminmoore.com

C2 Paint
c2paint.com

California Paints
californiapaints.com

Chateau Domingue
chateaudomingue.com

Donald Kaufman Color
donaldkaufmancolor.com

Eve Ashcraft Studio
eveashcraft.com

Farrow & Ball
farrow-ball.com

Fine Paints of Europe
finepaintsofeurope.com

CUSTOM FURNITURE
AND SPECIALTY
MILLWORK

Anthony Lawrence-Belfair
anthonylawrence.com

Blatt Billiards
blattbilliards.com

Burden
jonathanburden.com

Charles H. Beckley
(custom mattresses and beds)
chbeckley.com

The Country Bed Shop
countrybedshop.com

The Federalist (beds)
thefederalistonline.com

Leonards New England
(antique reproduction beds)
leonardsnewengland.com

Reid Classics
(antique reproduction beds)
reidclassics.com

Sawkille Co.
sawkille.com

Thomas Newman Studio (cabinets)
thomasnewmanstudio.com

Yorkville Caning Furniture
Repair
yorkvillecaning.com

DECORATIVE LIGHTING

Akari Light Sculptures
shop.noguchi.org/collections/
akari-light-sculptures

Ann-Morris
ann-morris.com

Artsylights.com
artsylights.com

Cedric Hartman
cedrichartman.com

Charles Edwards
charlesedwards.com

Collier Webb
collierwebb.com

Galerie des Lampes
galeriedeslampes.com

Hector Finch
hectorfinch.com

Howe London
howelondon.com

Jamb
jamb.co.uk

McLean Lighting Works
mcleanlighting.com

Nesle
nesleinc.com

Paul Ferrante
paulferrante.com

Period Lighting Fixtures
periodlighting.com

Reborn Antiques
rebornantiques.net

Remains Lighting Company
remains.com

RH
restorationhardware.com

Robert Kime
robertkime.com

Scofield Lighting
hmwpa.com/scofield-lighting

Soane Britain
soane.com

Urban Archaeology
urbanarchaeology.com

The Urban Electric Co.
urbanelectric.com

Vaughan
vaughandesigns.com

Visual Comfort & Co.
visualcomfort.com

Waterworks
waterworks.com

DECORATIVE METALWORK AND FINISHING

Empire Metal
empiremetal.net

Les Métalliers Champenois
lesmetallierschampenois.com

DECORATIVE PAINTING, WOOD FINISHING, AND FURNITURE RESTORATION

Agustin Hurtado
www.instagram.com/chango-brooklyn/

Burden
jonathanburden.com

Fitzkaplan Restoration
fitzkaplan.com

Jean Carrau Interieurs
jeancarrau.com

DECORATIVE PLASTER AND SCAGLIOLA

Balmer Architectural Mouldings
(*plaster moldings and columns*)
balmer.com

David Flaharty, sculptor
(*plaster ceiling medallions*)
davidflaharty@comcast.net

Suleiman Studios (*scagliola and custom plaster elements*)
madya6@aol.com

DOOR, WINDOW, AND CABINET HARDWARE

Ball & Ball Hardware Reproductions
(*brass and wrought iron*)
ballandball.com

D.C. Mitchell
(*brass and wrought iron*)
dcmitchell.org

E. R. Butler & Co.
(*brass, nickel, bronze, and silver*)
erbutler.com

Folger + Burt Architectural Hardware (*brass, nickel, and bronze*)
folgerandburt.com

Frank Allart (*brass and nickel*)
allart.co.uk

H. Theophile (*brass, nickel, bronze, and silver*)
htheophile.com

Historic Housefitters Co.
(*hand-forged wrought iron*)
historichousefitters.com

Katonah Architectural Hardware (*brass, nickel, and bronze*)
katonahhardware.com

Nanz (*brass, nickel, bronze, and silver*)
nanz.com

Rocky Mountain Hardware
rockymountainhardware.com

Sun Valley Bronze (*forged bronze*)
sunvalleybronze.com

Whitechapel
whitechapel-ltd.com

FABRIC HOUSE FAVORITES

Arabel Fabrics
arabelfabrics.com

Bennison Fabrics
bennisonfabrics.com

C&C Milano
cec-milano.us

Chelsea Textiles
chelseatextiles.com

Claremont Furnishing Fabrics Company
claremontfurnishing.com

Clarence House
clarencehouse.com

Cowtan & Tout
cowtan.com

DeLany & Long
delanyandlong.com

Dualoy Leather
dualoy.com

Holland & Sherry
hollandandsherry.com

The House of Scalamandré
scalamandre.com

John Rosselli & Associates
johnrosselli.com

Kravet
kravet.com

Lee Jofa
kravet.com/lee-jofa

Les Indiennes
lesindiennes.com

Lewis & Wood
lewisandwood.co.uk

Loro Piana
loropiana.com/textile

Passementerie
Tel. 212-355-7600

Pierre Frey
pierrefrey.com

Quadrille
quadrillefabrics.com

Robert Kime
robertkime.com

Rogers & Goffigon
rogersandgoffigon.com

Rose Cumming | Classic Cloth
wellstextiles.com

Rose Tarlow Melrose House
rosetarlow.com

Samuel & Sons
samuelandsons.com

Sarajo
sarajo.com

Schumacher
fschumacher.com

Soane Britain
soane.co.uk

Suzanne Tucker Home
suzannetuckerhome.com

Svenskt Tenn
svenskttenn.com

FRAMERS

APF Munn Master Framemakers
apfmunn.com

Brentano's
brentanosinc.com

The House of Heydenryk
heydenryk.com

J. Pocker
jpocker.com

LAMPSHADES

Blanche Field
blanchefield.com

Edgar-Reeves Lighting
edgar-reeves.com

Just Shades
justlampshades.com

LINENS (BED AND TABLE)

The Company Store
thecompanystore.com

Garnet Hill
garnethill.com

Léron
leron.com

Matouk
matouk.com

Schweitzer Linen
schweitzerlinen.com

Sferra
sferra.com

PLUMBING FIXTURES,
FITTINGS, AND
BATH ACCESSORIES

Barber Wilsons & Co.
barwil.co.uk

Kallista
kallista.com

Lefroy Brooks
usa.lefroybrooks.com

Newport Brass
newportbrass.com

Samuel Heath
samuel-heath.com

Urban Archaeology
urbanarchaeology.com

The Water Monopoly
thewatermonopoly.com

Waterworks
waterworks.com

PORCH AND GARDEN
FURNITURE

Bamboo&Rattan
vintagebamboorattan.com

Barbara Israel Garden Antiques
bi-gardenantiques.com

Berkshire Home & Antiques
1stdibs.com/dealers/berkshire-
home-and-antiques/

Bielecky Brothers
bieleckybrothers.com

Corner House Antiques
americanantiquewicker.com

Country Casual Teak
countrycasualteak.com

Crate & Barrel
crateandbarrel.com

Hervé Baume
herve-baume.com

Janus et Cie
janusetcie.com

McKinnon and Harris
mckinnonharris.com

Munder Skiles
munder-skiles.com

Walters
walterswicker.com

STONE AND TILE

Ann Sacks
annsacks.com

Chateau Domingue
chateaudomingue.com

Exquisite Surfaces
xsurfaces.com

Natural Stone Resources
nsrstone.com

Nemo Tile
nemotile.com

Paris Ceramics
parisceramics.com

Solar Antique Tiles
solarantiquetiles.com

Stone Source
stonesource.com

Waterworks
waterworks.com

WALLPAPER (SCENIC,
BLOCK-PRINTED,
AND TEXTURED)

Adelphi Paper Hangings
adelphipaperhangings.com

Barkskin Wallcoverings
by Caba Company
barkskin.com

Blithfield
blithfield.co.uk

Cowtan & Tout
cowtan.com

de Gournay
degournay.com

Elizabeth Dow
elizabethdow.com

Galbraith & Paul
galbraithandpaul.com

George Spencer Designs
georgespencer.com

Hamilton Weston Wallpapers
hamiltonweston.com

Joanna Rock Wallpapers
Tel. 914-693-7699

Lee Jofa
kravet.com/lee-jofa

Marthe Armitage Prints
marthearmitage.co.uk

Peter Fasano
peterfasano.com

Phillip Jeffries
phillipjeffries.com

Robert Kime
robertkime.com

WINDOWS AND
GLASS DOORS

Dover Windows & Doors
doverwindows.com

Hope's
hopeswindows.com

Jada
jadawindows.com

Little Harbor Window Company
littleharborwindow.com

Marvin
marvin.com

Oliveri Millworks
oliverimillworks.com

Pella
pella.com

Reilly Architectural
reillyarch.com

Stewart Brannen Millworks
brannenmillwork.com

West Coast Architectural
Millwork
westcoastam.com

ACKNOWLEDGMENTS

For the twenty-plus years that I've had my firm, so many talented, extraordinary people have had a hand in the work that we've done—as well as in the sharing of that work with the world. To each and every one, I owe a huge debt of gratitude.

At the top of that list have been the amazing group of architects, designers, and our administrative team that have been the heart and soul of my firm, G. P. Schafer Architect, since its founding in 2002. That group begins with my partner, Lou Taylor, and our original studio director and principal, Mickey Benson, and includes studio directors Carl Carfi, Matt Enquist, and Laura Welsh, associate Chris Taylor, as well as Amy Agne, Andrew Almeida, Tom Ambler, Thomas Assad, Sara Barsoom, Margaret Bartenstein, Ann Barton, Sean Blackwell, Laura Blochwitz, Keaton Bloom, Thomas Boyle, Aimee Buccellato, Kevin Buccellato, Ali Buersmeyer, Erin Burke, Michael Callaway, Jack Calvert, Daniela Cascio, Bryan Cates, Iris Cerezo, Alejandra Cesar, Maria Cruz, Christopher D'Amico, Micah Dawson, Sheila Delaney, Brad Devendorf, George Distefano, Rachel Edelstein, Whitley Esteban, Emily Fuchs, Tessa Gearity, Michael Geller, Sarah Gumenick, John Hanlon, Parker Hansen, Michael Harris, Matthew Hayes, Katrina Hendricks, Amanda Holenstein, Benjamin Hoyumpa, Ryan Hughes, Holly Johnson, Maggie Jones, Hope Kenny, Catherine Kirchhoff, Whitney Kirk, Josh Kleinberg, Michelle Lamontagne, Matthew Leonard, Mary Grace Lewis, Teresa Lopes, Monica Luca, Sarah MacWright, Ian Manire, Tyler Many, Nick Markovich, Cecilia McCammon, Brendan McNee, Paige Melinis, Michael Mesko, Samuel Methvin, Nick Meury, Teresa Michailovs, Jheanelle Miller, Ellen Mitchell, Tony Moniaga, Benjamin Moore, Chris Moran, Elaine Moran, Molua Muldown, Stefanie Mustian, Andrey Nash, Khara Nemitz, Lilian Niewald, Frank Noska IV, Eduardo Oronia, Lenore Passavanti, Julia Pesola, Joseph Peterson, Sarah Pisano, Mark Pledger, Austin Proehl, Darin Quan, Jahlay Rae, J. D. Ramirez, Manny Ramirez, Jr., Jessica Rausch, Danielle Reed, Vladimir Reed, Rachel Reilly, Diana Reising, Kayla Rembold, Natasha Rivera, Danny Sacco, Anika Sanchez-Piotrowski, Eero Schultz, Lyndsey Segond, Benjamin Sessa, Benjamin Shelton, David Sobol, Philip Spence, Brina Stachecki, Dylan Sullivan, Manuel Tan, Andy Taylor, Tori Thorgersen, Jean-Marie Truchard, Christine Valiquette, Joseph Vega, Erica Verbeek, Riccardo Vicenzino, Olivia Voytovich, Liam Walsh, Christopher Whelan, J. Ryan White, Matthew Winter, Sharon Wong, Isabella Zayas, Caroline Zorc. Each has made important contributions to our vision of what living beautifully can mean to a homeowner today, not to mention the quality of the work we have produced as a result of that vision.

My appreciation also extends to the numerous and brilliant interior designers, landscape designers, engineers, consultants, builders, artisans, and craftspeople with whom we've had the distinct privilege of collaborating over the years, and who have brought both new dimensions and consistent excellence to each of our projects.

I must also thank the many editors and writers who have believed in our work and exposed it so generously to their readers over the decades, as well as the gifted image-makers and stylists who have photographed our projects in ways that so beautifully captured the quality of life that we hope all of our clients enjoy in the homes we design.

Additionally, I must express my immense gratitude to the many exceptional clients with whom the firm has collaborated since we opened our doors. In the beginning, we were delighted that anyone would take a chance on us; later, we were grateful for those who had the faith, patience, and vision to push us in ever more challenging—and inspiring—new directions. We are deeply appreciative, not only for the assignments we've received, but the memories and dreams that have motivated them—the stories our clients told, the aspirations they expressed, and the hopes they shared. The emotional aspects of our work are as important as the practical ones—if not more so—and for the clients who have entrusted us with these gifts we remain profoundly thankful.

Lastly, my note of thanks would be incomplete without acknowledging the incredible team with whom I have worked for the last fifteen years on my three books. To Charles Miers, who first saw the possibility of a story my work could tell; to my editor at Rizzoli, Kathleen Jayes, who helped me always keep that story on track; to my endlessly amusing and inspired co-writer, Marc Kristal, who gave me the words to tell my stories more eloquently; to my brilliant photographic partners in crime—Eric Piasecki for the images and Helen Crowther for the style; to Doug Turshen and Steve Turner, who have deftly and beautifully crafted these three books; to John Hanlon in my office, who tirelessly and with good humor always kept the trains running, and on time; to Tom Maciag, who for the last two decades has been my vitally important partner, alongside the production of these three books, in creating every other piece of graphics my office has shared in print and on-line; to Sarah Burningham, who has been my extraordinary little bird with the big impact; and lastly to Jill Cohen, who helped me find the story of my work in the first place and then sorted out how to tell it in a way that would resonate. To each and every one of you I am deeply grateful.

In the end, this book has been about the journey of life and how that can deepen your understanding of the work you do each day. And for that I am most grateful for my own family: Courtnay, Bankes, and Bennett. How wonderful it is to truly feel home, at last!

First published in the United States of America in 2024 by
Rizzoli International Publications, Inc.
300 Park Avenue South
New York, NY 10010
www.rizzoliusa.com

Text: Marc Kristal
All photographs by Eric Piasecki except:
Page 10: Photo courtesy of the author
Page 12-13: Photo by Simon Upton
Page 254 : Top photo: "Borland Yacht Monaloa"; Courtesy of the Ken
Carlson Collection at the Camden Public Library. Bottom photo:
"Monaloa on the Rails"; Courtesy of the Harry Smith Collection at the
Camden Public Library.
Page 328: Photo courtesy of G. P. Schafer, Architect

Publisher: Charles Miers
Senior Editor: Kathleen Jayes
Design: Doug Turshen and Steve Turner
Production Manager: Colin Hough Trapp
Managing Editor: Lynn Scrabis

Developed in collaboration with Jill Cohen Associates, LLC.

Printed in China

2024 2025 2026 2027 / 10 9 8 7 6 5 4 3 2

ISBN: 978-0-8478-9978-4

Library of Congress Control Number: 2023945157

Visit us online:
Facebook.com/RizzoliNewYork
Twitter: @Rizzoli_Books
Instagram.com/RizzoliBooks
Pinterest.com/RizzoliBooks
Youtube.com/user/RizzoliNY
Issuu.com/Rizzoli

PREVIOUS PAGE: In a boathouse in Maine, one of the many singular
and delightful emblems of a lifetime of collecting by my clients.

PAGES 2-3: A family compound in Vermont, on a promontory
overlooking Lake Champlain, enjoys views of the water
and the Adirondack mountains.

PAGE 5: A sun-dappled tableau suggests the pleasures of Down East
living in a house on the coast of Maine.

PAGE 6: One of a pair of American Federal-style mantelpieces we
designed for the living room of a family compound on Long Island.

FRONT JACKET PHOTO: Sunlight streams into a glazed porch in a
Colonial Revival house on Long Island.

REAR JACKET PHOTO: A spectacular water view greets visitors to this
new house on the shores of Lake Champlain in Vermont.